WILD AND FREE
HORSES OF THE OUTER BANKS

Book, Text, and Photographs Copyright © 2015 Garrett Fisher. All rights reserved.

Maps Copyright © OpenStreetMap contributors. Map data, including map modifications made by the author, is available under the Open Database License, cartography licensed as CC-BY-SA. Please see openstreetmap.org, opendatacommons.org, and creativecommons.org.

ISBN: 0692408703
ISBN-13: 978-0692408704

Published by Tenmile Publishing LLC - Alpine, WY
Website & Blog: garrettfisher.me

All photos in this book are available as prints, digital files, and framed prints. Please visit the website.

Table of Contents

Somehow I Thought I Didn't Like Horses	8
Corolla, NC - Where the Horses Live	14
Living with the Horses	26
Horse Photography Tips	39
The Future of the Horses	45
Visiting the Horses	78
About the Author	80

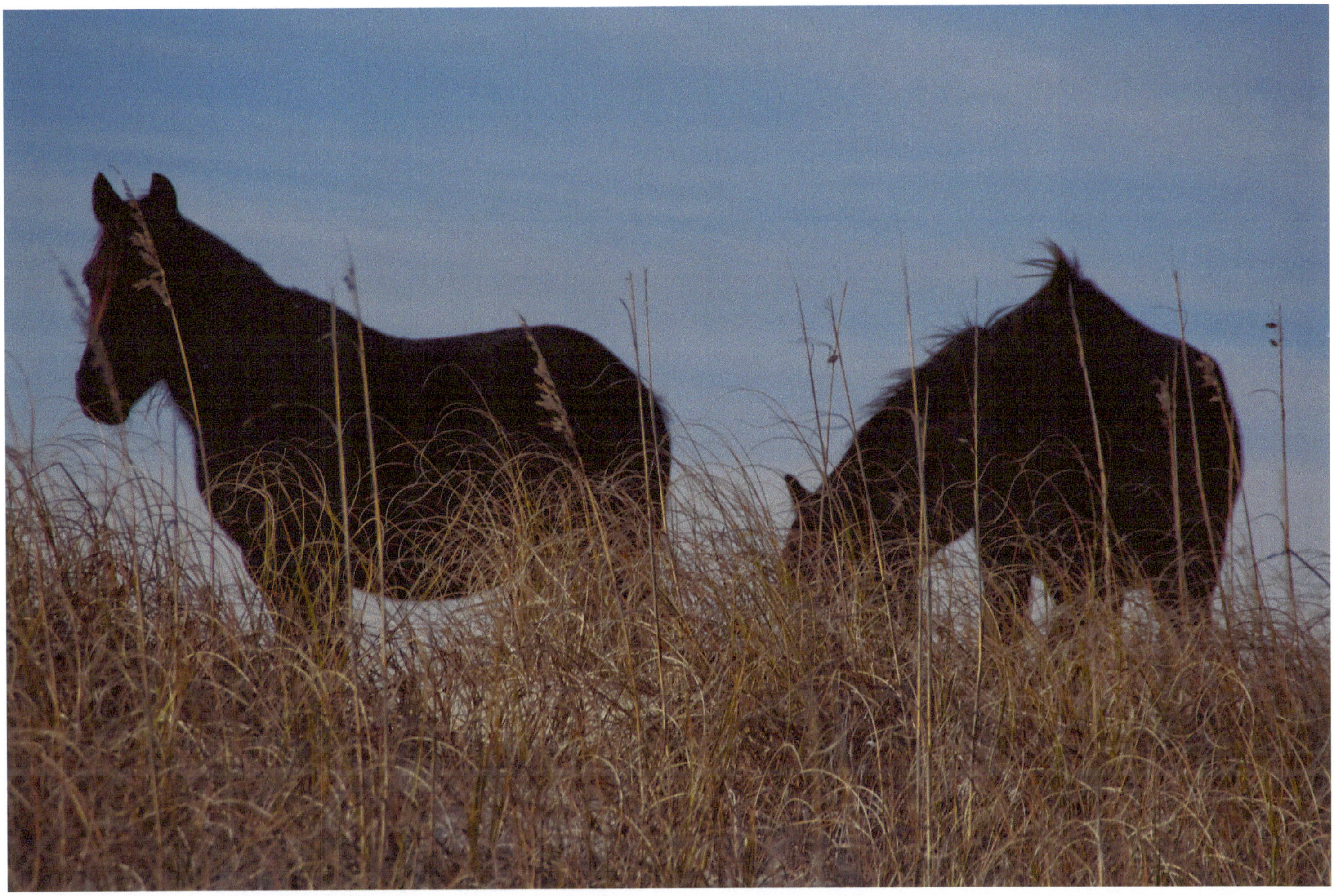

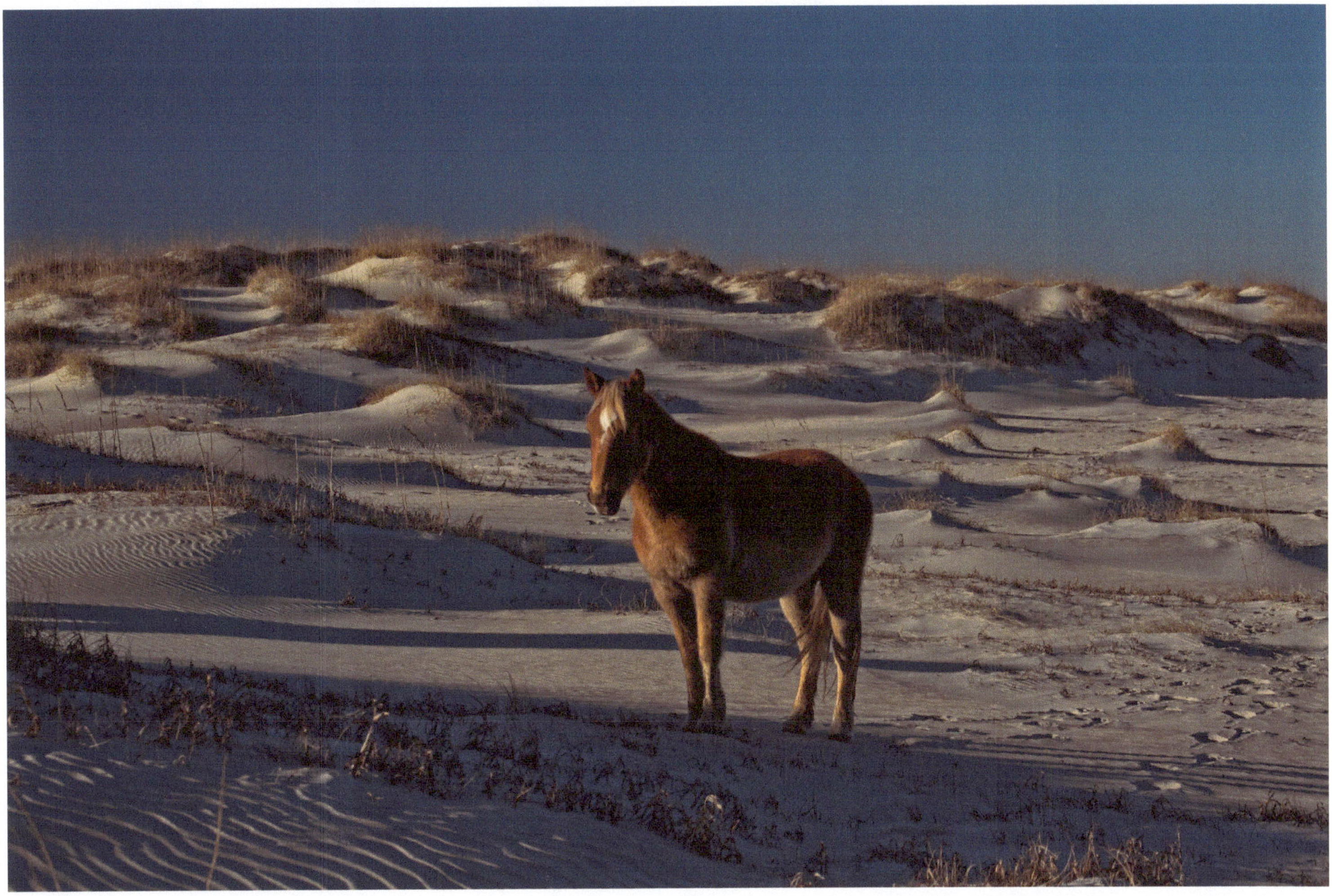

Somehow I Thought I Didn't Like Horses

It would seem kind of odd if I told you that I thought I did not even like horses before putting this book together. I had taken two horse rides in my life: one as a young teenager, and another just short of turning 20. The first ride clearly gave away that I knew nothing of horses, as the primary takeaway was that horses have a mind of their own, and I wondered why someone would saddle themselves to an enormous animal that seems intent on doing what it wants. My second ride only worsened my distrust, as I rented a horse while doing non-profit work in Ecuador, only to realize that the saddle did not come with stirrups, and I was and am far too sizable of an American to simply squeeze my legs into the horse's rib cage in order to make the ride, shall we say, less painful. The horse knew I was incompetent, and registered its displeasure by attempting to hurl me off of a seaside cliff. At that moment, I simply wrote off the whole horse thing as something that would best be avoided.

Eight years after the misunderstanding with the South American horse, I was introduced to the wild horses in Corolla. Horses living on the beach, wild, now that was something that had an immediate connection, on a deep level. There was something about them, being wild first of all, and on the frontier of human civilization, living on shifting sands, surf, and wind that was hopelessly attractive.

As the fall of 2014 approached, a work contract came to an end, and we had the opportunity to leave the bustle of the city and go elsewhere. While we wanted to go to the Rockies, it was the beginning of the ski season, and that is a poor time to make a move of that significance. I floated the idea that we should spend the winter in the Outer Banks, as we both had always wanted to live by the ocean. It was obvious that we had to live in the 4x4 section of Corolla, amongst the horses. It didn't take but a moment for me to decide that I would spend the winter getting to know the wild horses, photographing them, and eventually sharing my work in a book.

Even as we arrived and I giddily scampered about taking photos multiple times per day, I still felt that I did not have the same infatuation with horses that most people do. The majority of young girls want a pony, and horse riding seems to be popular enough, yet I couldn't identify my-

self with the horse lover crowd. I even made a comment to my wife, after a long photo shoot: "I don't even like horses." She replied: "You should hear how you talk about them."

That got me thinking. Clearly, she had to be right, as I had, in fact, moved to the coast to see them, and was writing a book about them. I talked to my grandfather about the subject, and he pointed out that the horses were living as they should be, entirely free. I mentioned that they had a nice life, though if someone feeds and takes care of a horse that has a large pasture to enjoy, it also lives a charmed life. "Nope, that's not right. The horse needs to be free," he replied. At that moment, I remembered a conversation I had with my grandfather after my grandmother in no uncertain terms advised me of the rules that their dog must be blocked from sleeping on the couch. After she left the room, he said: "Grandma doesn't seem to want the dog on the couch. As far as I am concerned, if the dog wants to sleep on the couch, he can." That conversation, coupled with a very similar discussion with my wife about our overly enterprising canine resulted in an epiphany: I thought I did not like horses because the only horses I had ever seen were living in captivity. I like wild horses! I had gotten this idea from my grandfather, that animals should be free, and for the first time, I found horses that were truly wild and free.

It did not take long before I got the hang of where to find the horses, and to understand what their moods were. The more time went by, the more we seemed to develop a mutual understanding, as it became evident to me that the horses would rather not be swarmed by tourists; they would much rather that those observing them do so quietly and respectfully, akin to how one would imagine a wildlife photographer in Africa keeping his or her impact as minimal as possible. It seemed that the horses appreciated when they were respected. Over time, I developed quite an attachment to them, missing them when I was away for a few days, and dreaming about some of them.

Even now as the busy season arrived and we had to take our leave from the coast, I am living in horse country in Wyoming, where there are wild horse herds, pastured horses in abundance, and even a guy riding a horse on the state license plate. I am still trying to get my head around the idea of taking riding lessons, or maybe spending a significant amount of time with the wild horses here in the West. What path I take remains to be seen, though I can now truly say that I absolutely love them.

Left: *Eating some sea oats under full moon light.*

Corolla, NC - Where the Horses Live

When people hear about or visit the wild horses in Corolla, it is obvious from the looks on their faces that they know they are experiencing something unique and special. While the bulk of visitors savor the experience, stay a short while, and leave, I found myself determined to understand what about Corolla makes them so attractive, that they stir our souls in a way that words do not describe. After all, there are wild horses on the beach in Assateague, Maryland, Sapelo Island, Georgia, and Shackleford Banks, North Carolina, and those places don't quite capture the same mystique as Corolla.

It occurred to me about a month after moving to the beach why Corolla is different. It is the only place in the United States that I know of where people are able to live with wild horses. In fact, living with anything wild at all isn't very common. It seems to be that, here in America, we push away or extermi-

Above:

Aerial view of the 4x4 beach access ramp, where NC 12 leaves the pavement and becomes sand. Currituck Sound visible in the background.

Right:

Aerial photos of horses in Corolla, both on the ocean side and on the marsh side of the island.

nate wildlife that is annoying or perceived to be dangerous, and we relegate them to wilderness areas where we may only visit, we're not allowed to live there. Some places in the West have grown so much that national forests abut city limits, and a variety of wildlife can be found roaming where one does not expect. Otherwise, we don't really have towns where wildlife may roam the streets, places were lovers of those kinds of animals can choose to live with them. Culturally, animals belong in the wild, and people belong in civilization, and rarely shall the two mix, except in the zoo.

The story of Corolla is a long one, filled with a healthy dose of chance mixing with some dedicated people who have kept the horses from disappearing. A byproduct of an odd mix of government land ownership and government willingness to let the Corolla beach suffice for a highway long ago when next to

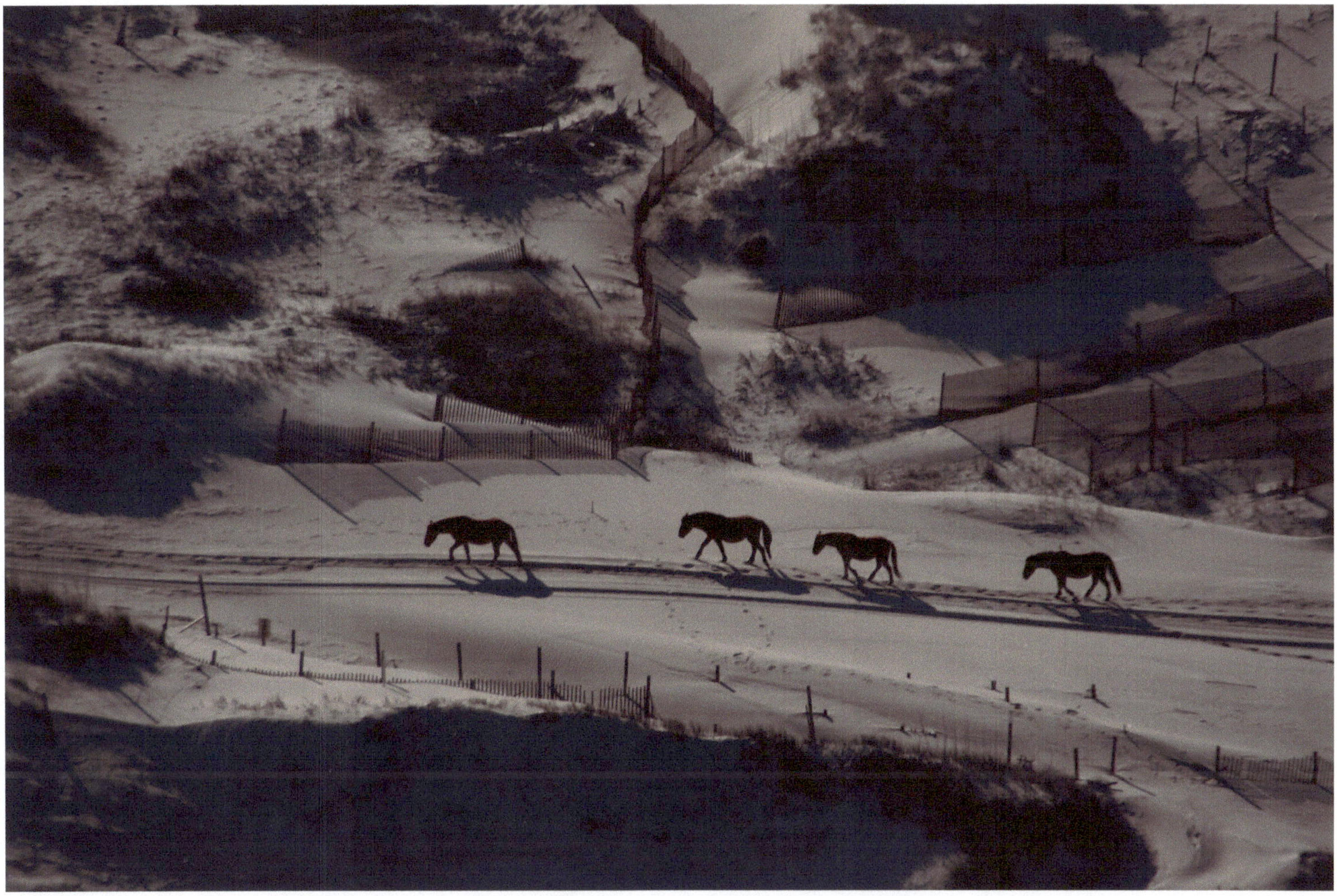

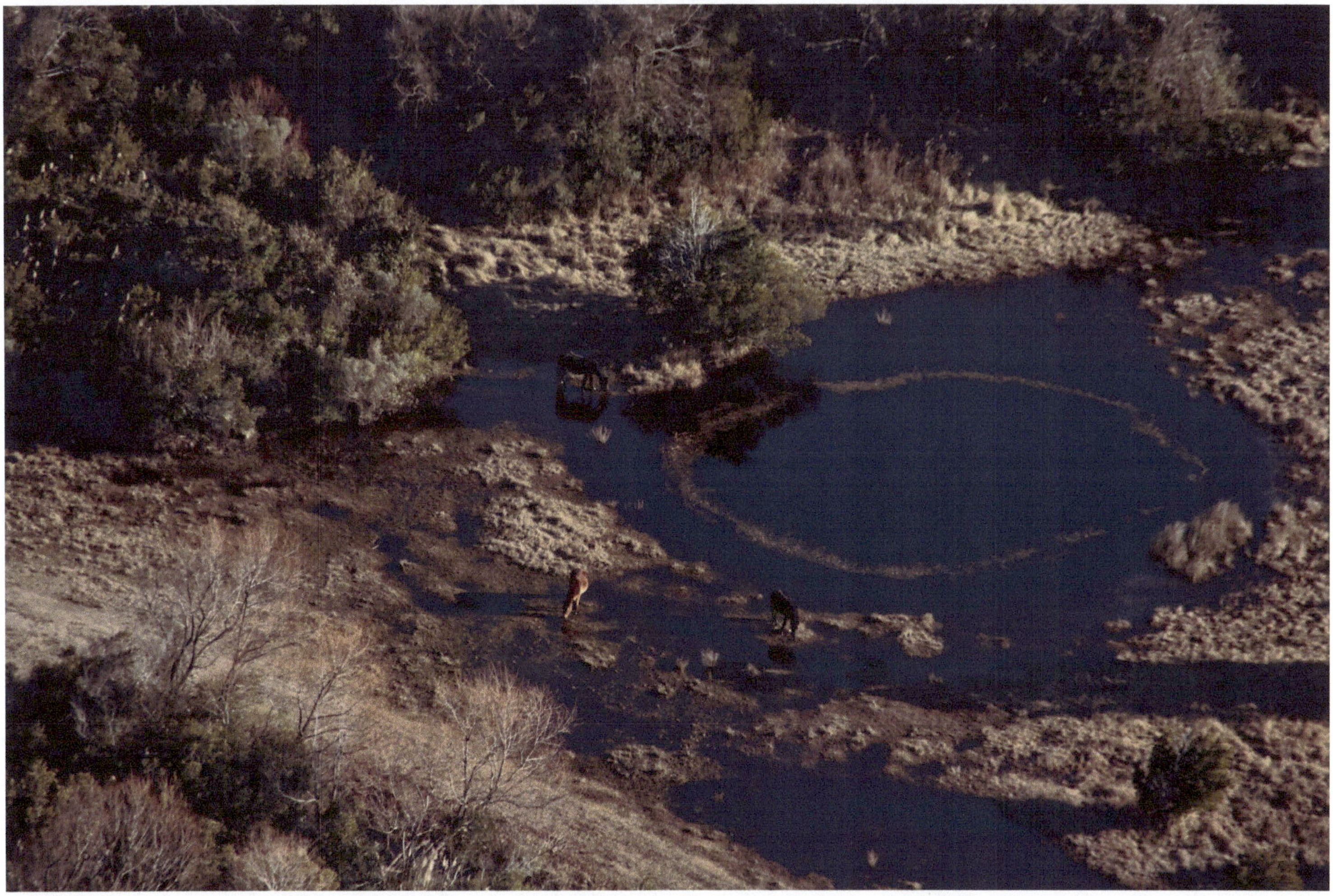

no one lived here, a one-of-a-kind place came to fruition where near mansions have been built in a rugged, dead end, remote place where the streets are made of sand, the highway is the beach, and there are no businesses. Corolla feels like the end of the earth, in a good kind of way, and the horses have coincidentally ridden the wave, coexisting side by side with large homes, parkland, tourists with vehicles stuck in the sand, and devoted longtime locals, living on a manmade frontier.

For those who have never been to Corolla, it is located at the far northern end of the Outer Banks, north of Kitty Hawk and Duck. NC highway 12 is the only access point, and it travels a good distance north before the highway unceremoniously becomes the beach. Turning a mere 300 feet to the right, suddenly one finds themselves passing over a livestock grate in the road (to keep the horses where they belong) and on the access ramp to the beach. From there, it is roughly 13 miles along the beach, about a

ABOVE:

Yes, they drink salt water.

LEFT:

Shackleford Banks - aerial, south of the Outer Banks, the source of "Gus," the stallion recently introduced with fresh genes.

third of it parkland, until reaching the Virginia border, where vehicle traffic is not allowed, and a sizable fence exists to keep the horses in North Carolina. Part non-profit, federal, state, and private land, this mixture of parcels has the commonality that the horses roam all of it.

As I will discuss in a future chapter, the horses are under constant threat, from small day-to-day things resulting from human ignorance, to governmental ambivalence, real estate interests, and political disinterest. What will save this utterly unique arrangement where majestic animals live side by side with humans along a beautiful coastline, will be a determined love of them by many people, and the determination to do what it takes to keep them right here, where they belong, wild and free, for all of us to enjoy.

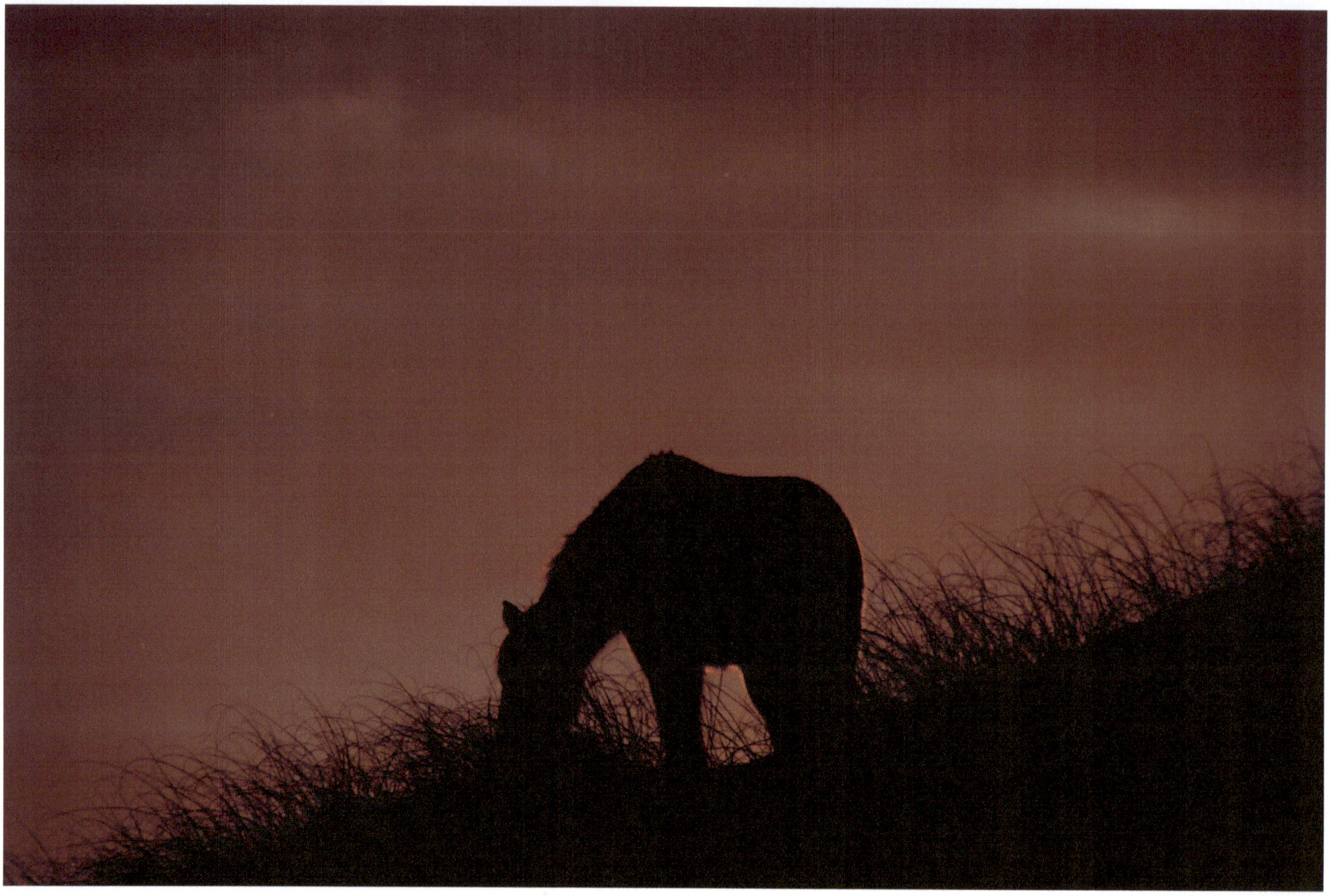

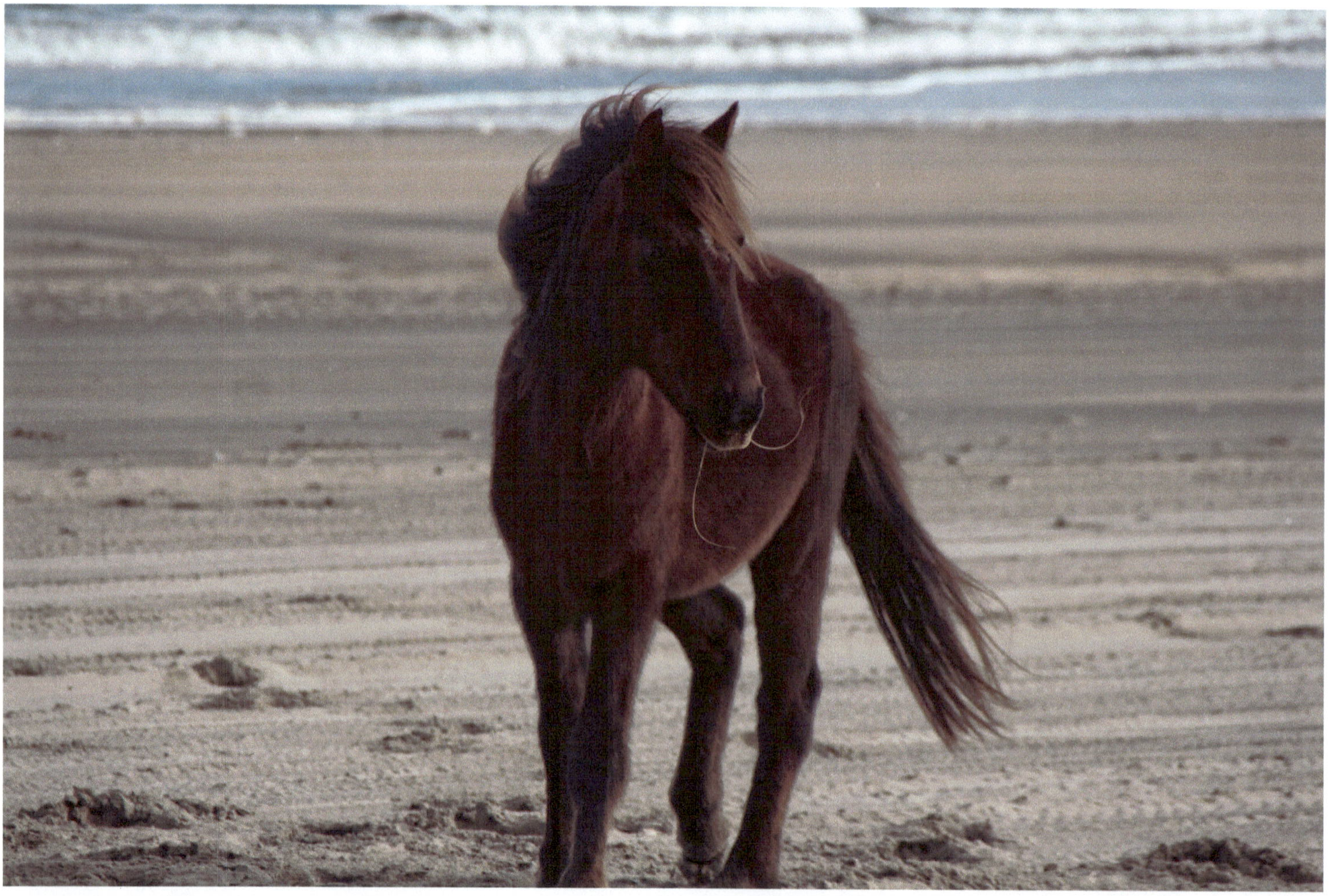

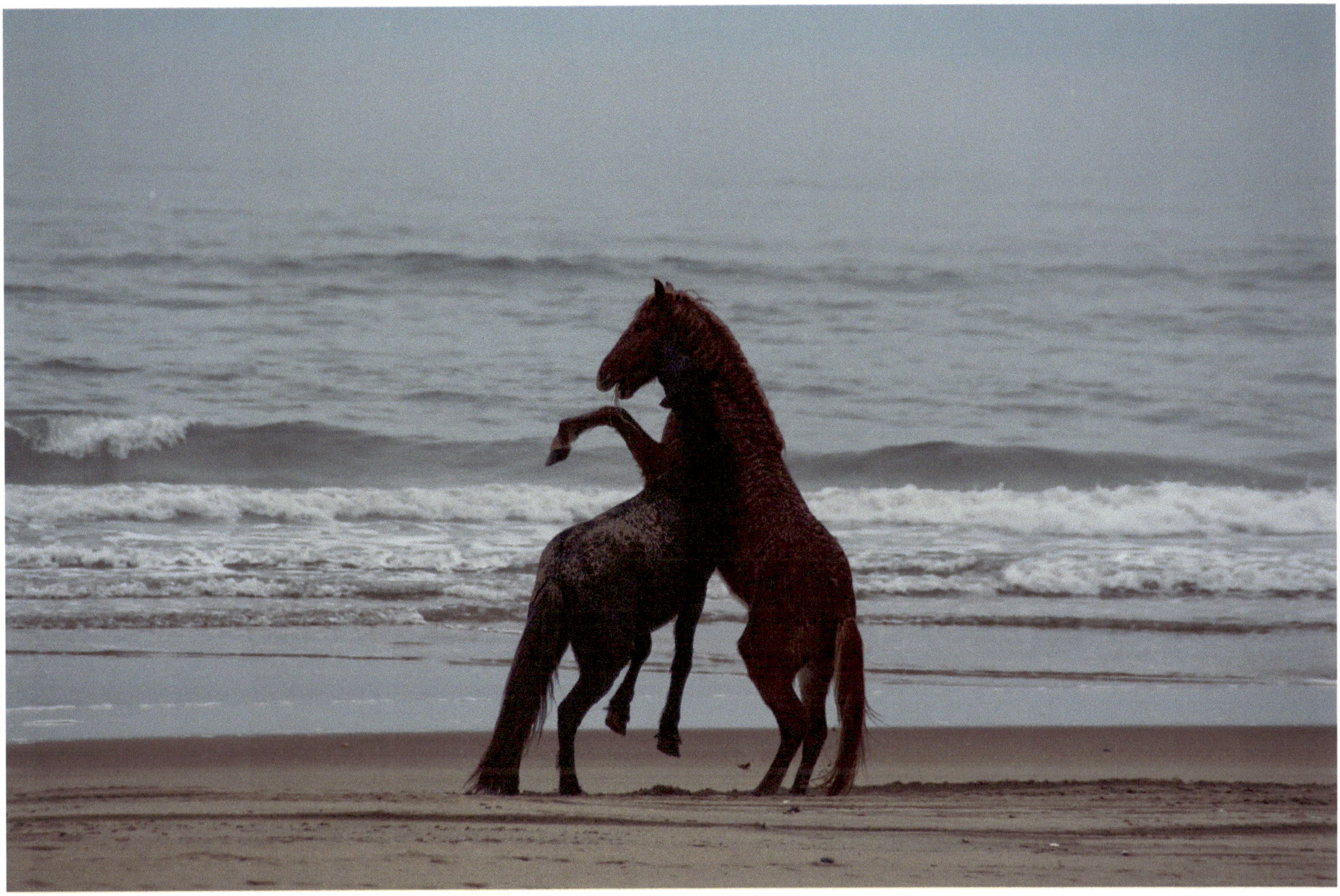

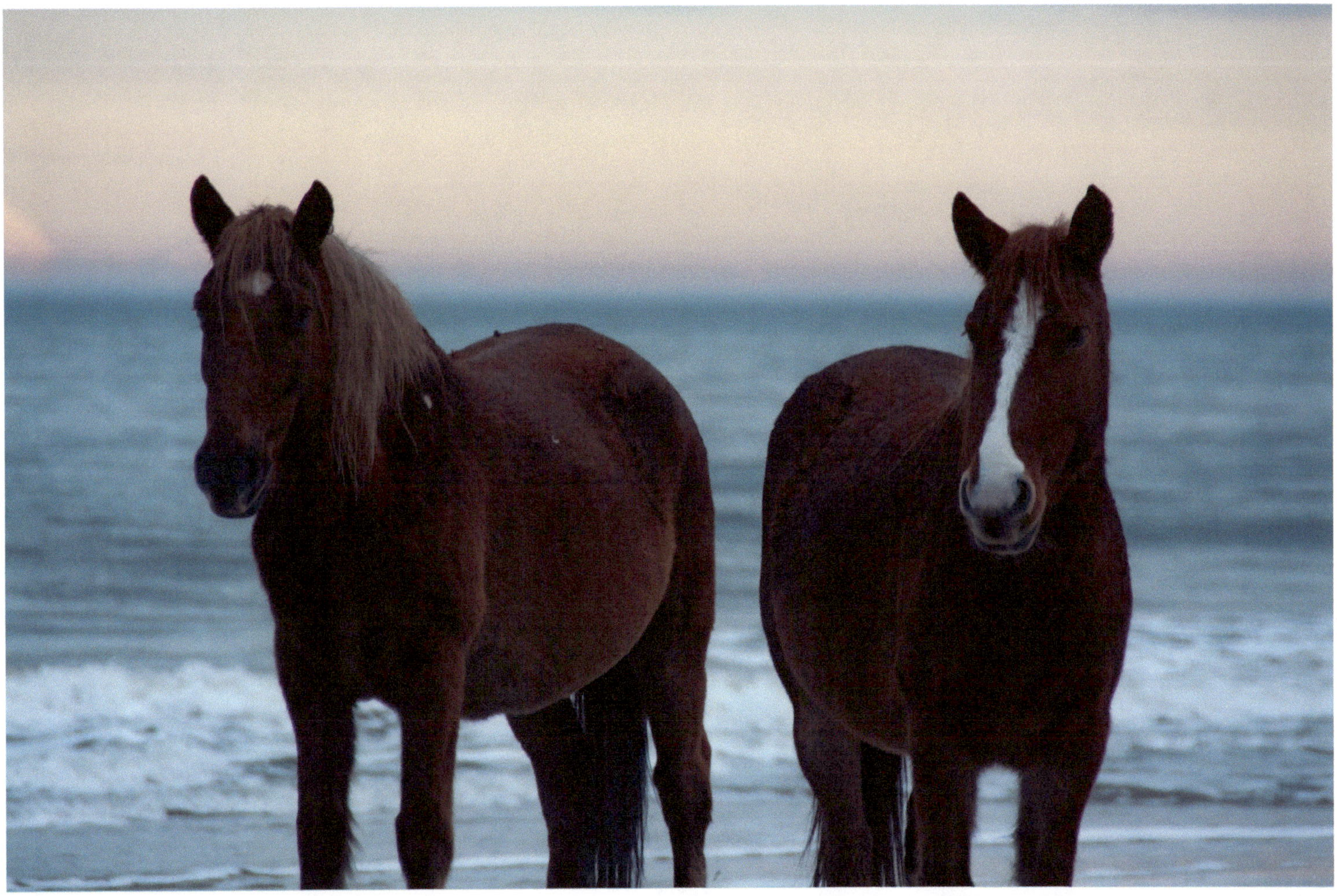

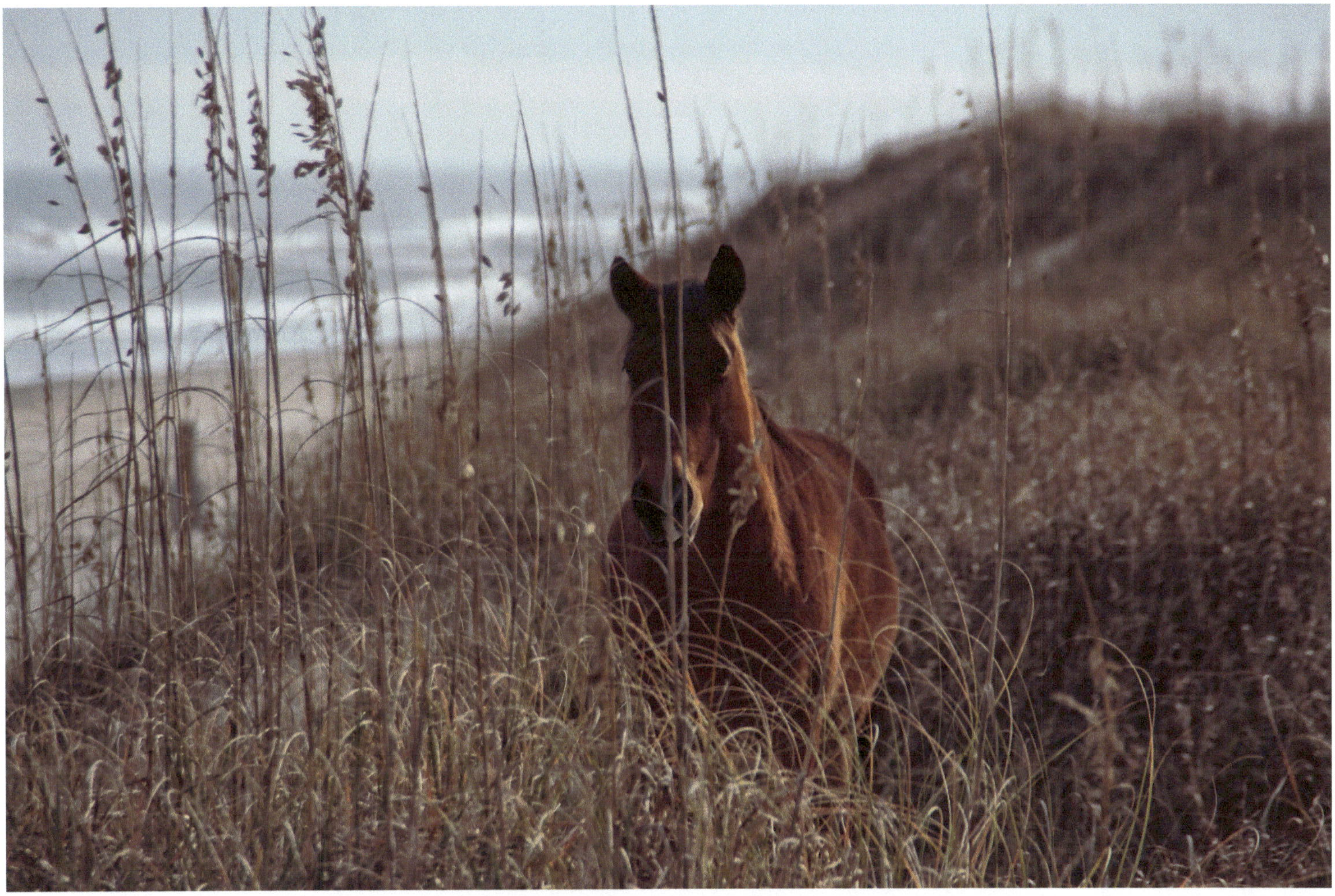

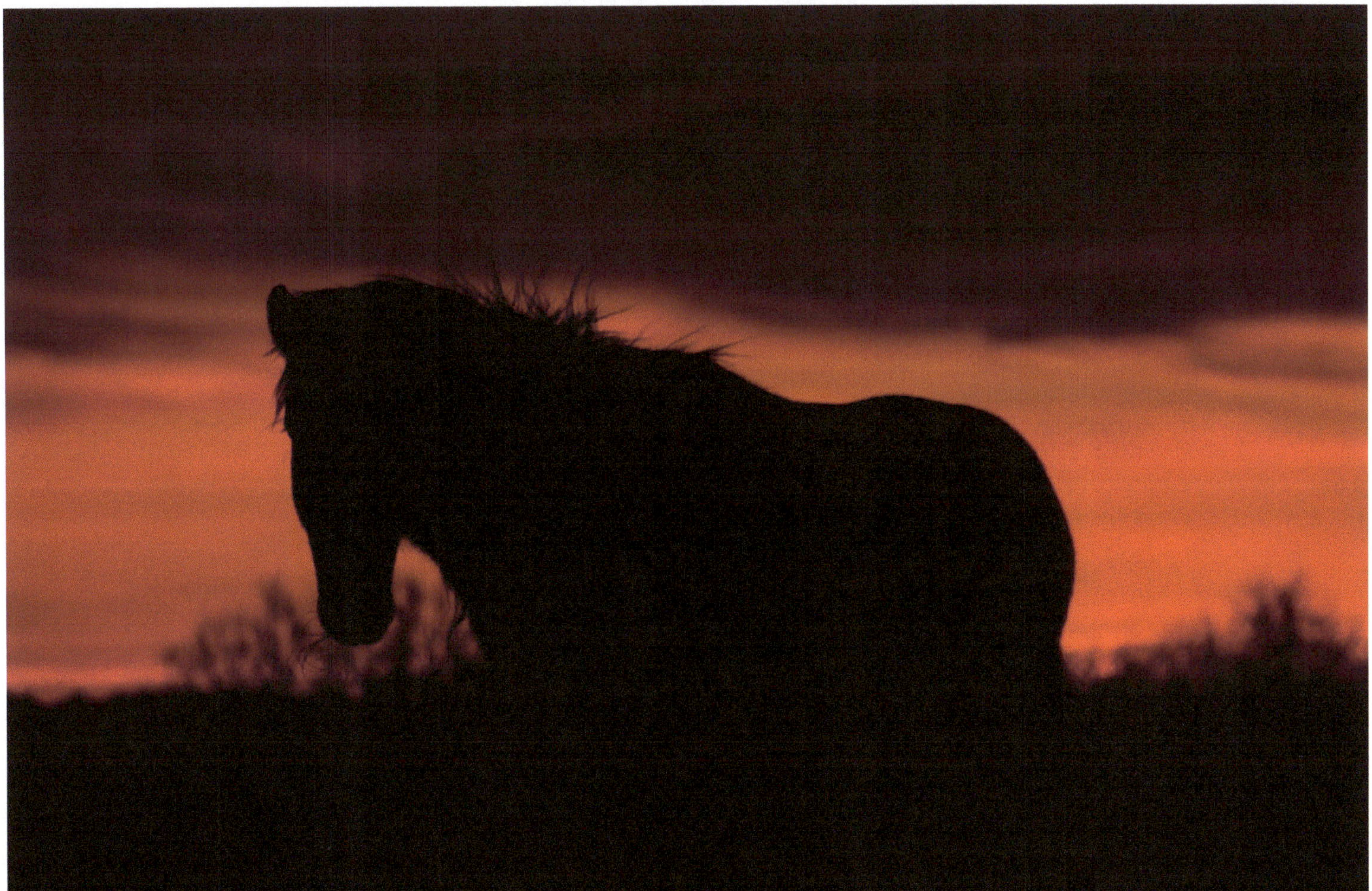

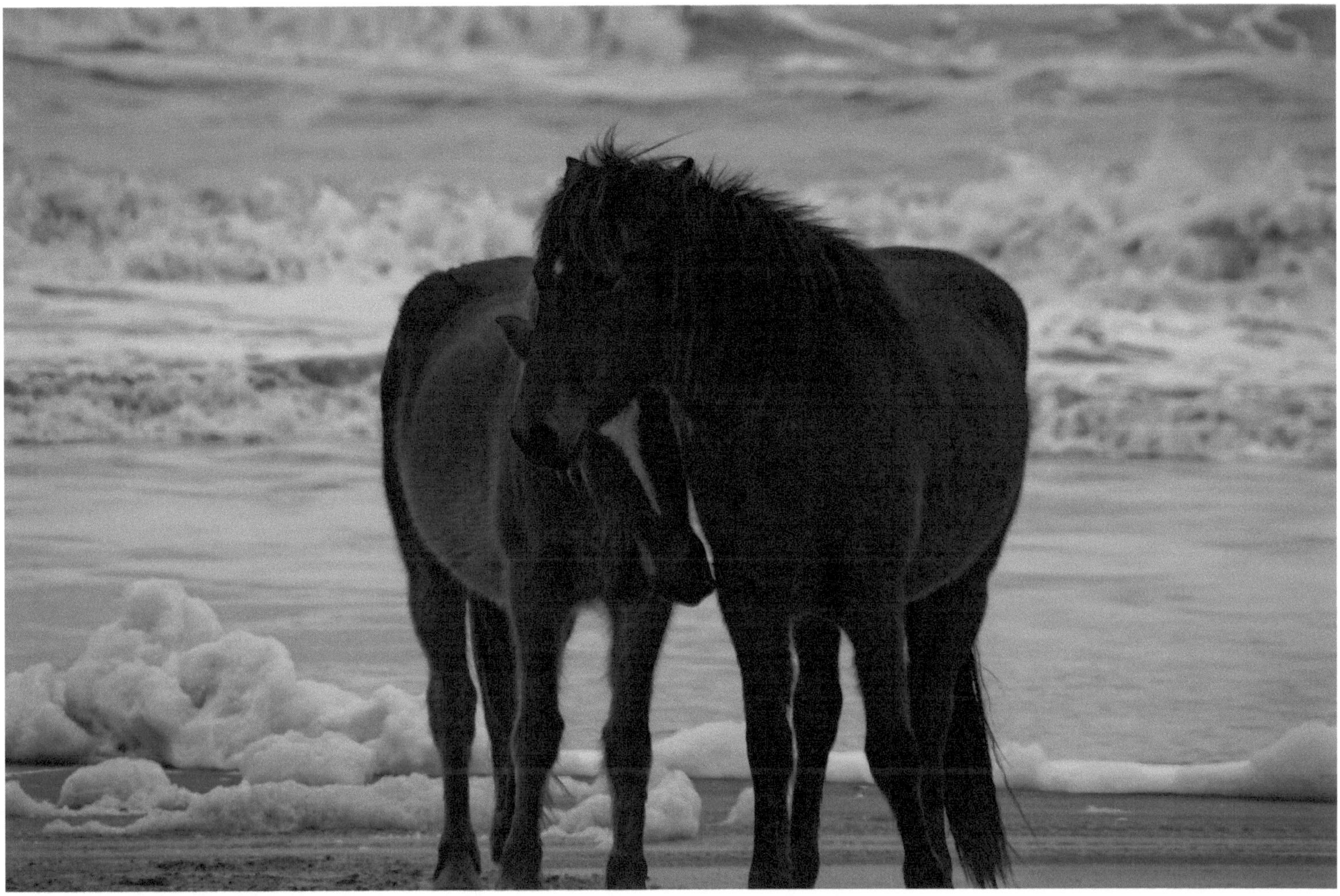

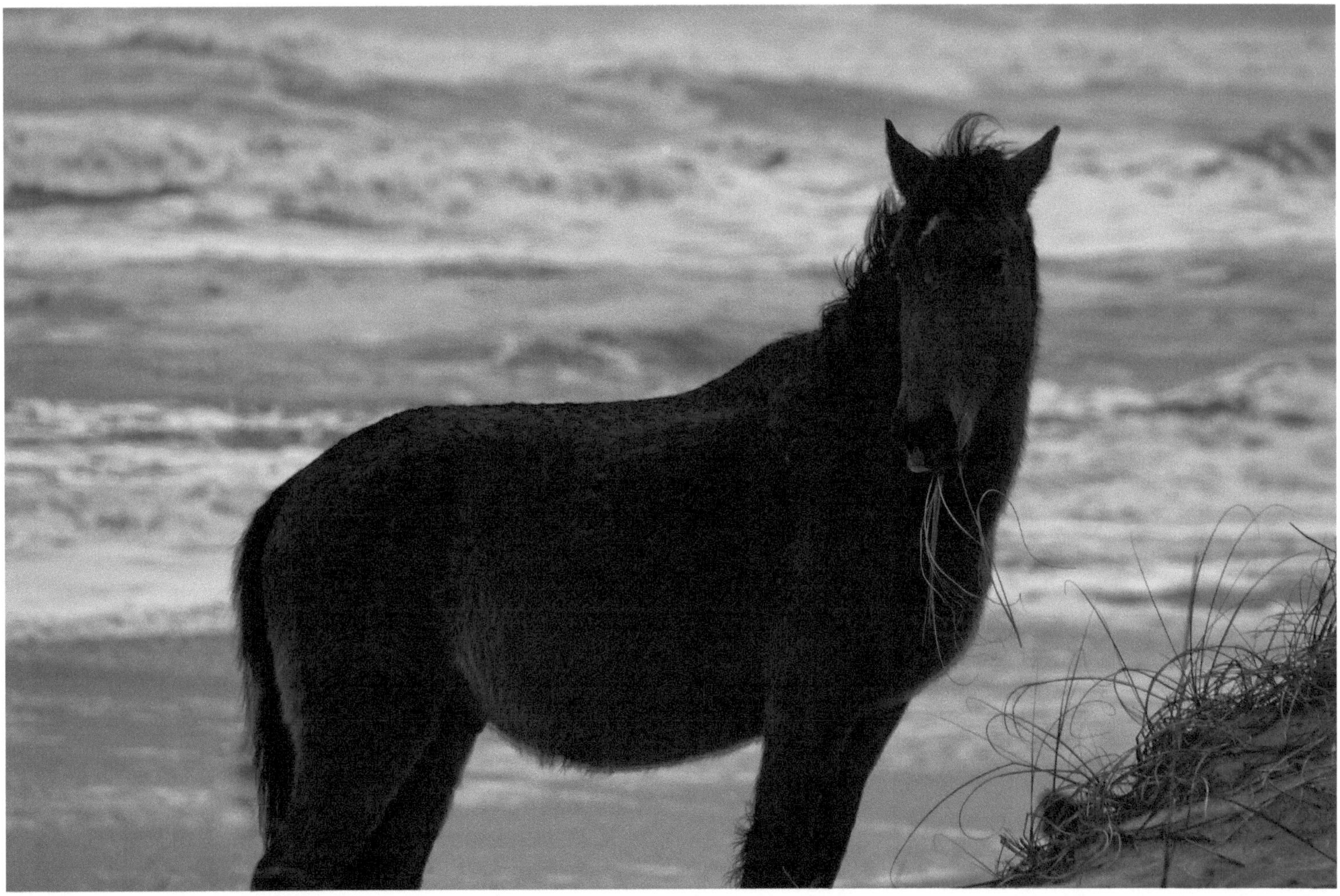

Living with the Horses

I can definitely say that I did not know what to expect when it came to spending an entire winter with the horses. My experience to date had been that the horses seemed to have an agenda to hide from humans, making only occasional appearances and otherwise being a frustration. It took some time to understand what motivates them, and therefore to figure out their routines. I simply thought I would be happy if I could find them on a regular basis.

The wild horses do not like to be gawked at by a crowd of people holding cameras. In my initial enthusiasm when I would see them, I looked like any old tourist, awkwardly standing there snapping away with a camera, while the horses turned the other way and ate grass or trudged their way up the beach, with wandering hoof prints going where I think not even they know. After awhile, I began to notice that many of the horses would turn away as soon as they heard the shutter of the camera, almost with a look of annoyance; yet, if I was respectful in my positioning, they would continue what they were doing. In other words, if they were aware I existed, yet I largely stood in some bushes or behind something, they were happier. If I awkwardly faced them in a wide-open spot, they seemed to turn the other way, as though I was invading space that they considered theirs. In my initial touristy glee to even see them, I failed to take note that I was entering their home, and they just might have some feelings about it.

As time went on, I began to notice that they had quite a number of predictable routines. To begin with, horses are territorial. Groups of horses stay together and operate in a relatively routine place. If you're observant, you'll see the same horses in the same areas. Secondly, they modulate their behaviors based on the weather. As they live outside, they have to manage rain, wind, cold, sun, heat, drinking water, and eating. As the 2014-2015 winter was the coldest since 1934, we had plenty of raw and cold days where the horses disappeared to the maritime forests, followed by time on the beach when the water was warmer and the sun stronger. In busier times, I would see them out on the beach during a full moon night, yet they might have been curiously absent during the day. Each encounter proved that they had more and more layers to their complexity.

ABOVE:

Horse yawning a few times in succession.

If the horses are going to lay down and nap, they like a day with minimal wind and some sun, and a few of them will choose a protected spot facing the sun. If you're fortunate enough to see it, they can be startled easily, and will likely only lay on their stomach, reserving lying on their side to very private places where another horse is with them. The only time I saw a horse lay on her side and put her head down was in the yard where we were living, and I could only photo her by sneaking extremely quietly onto the third floor balcony and quietly getting some shots. As soon as traffic went by on the street, she was sitting back up.

Their routine consists mostly of eating, with occasional interspersed naps, time on the beach, playing, and fighting. Eating is the mainstay of the herd's behavior, with grasses being the dominant food source, though they will nibble on vines and assorted other foliage. Mating rituals and territorial disputes will introduce rivalry among the stallions, and they go through any number of forms of expressing their discontent with each other, from noisy whinnying to kicking and outright biting and fighting. Females also enter into disagreements, though the outcome looks more playful and less nasty than males.

As to what drives them to the beach, it is hard to pinpoint. They tend to wander their way down the dune line, and then onto the beach, where they will play, fight, drink salt water, roll around on their backs to itch themselves, usually followed by a period that I call "trudging" where they aimlessly wander as a group, in a lethargic walk, sometimes for miles before returning to the dunes. In the summer, time on the beach is more scientific, as they are hot or are trying to ward off insects due to a breeze from the mainland.

Living with them on shared property is another story. Horses pretty much do what they want, so one day they might be hanging out under your house, and another they are grazing in the dark when its time to take the dog out. That is, needless to say, a highly interesting surprise. I was surprised out of my wits a number of nights, where horses were grazing a few feet from the road, hiding in the pitch dark, and a noise or two from them would be incredibly alarming for me and the dog. In the end, all of the drama was quite funny and we enjoyed it greatly. Sharing the beach with the horses is practically a spiritual experience. As it is, the ocean and crashing surf stir some-

thing inside of us, as we sit on the edge of human civilization and stare into something raw, beautiful, inviting, and yet terrifying. We want to swim in the ocean, yet we fear what it can do. Likewise, horses stir something deep in our soul, a reminder of a raw freedom that seems to have gotten away from our society. Horses are majestic and beautiful, strong yet calm. Mixing this symbol of freedom, the wild horse, with the magnitude of the ocean is an experience that is very hard to describe in words. Inasmuch as I would spend hours staring at the crashing waves, I would gaze at the horses, trying to soak up as much of both as I could, yet knowing that attempting to contain either the ocean or the horses would ruin it. Both of those things are what they are to us because they are left alone, unrestricted, wild, and free. We can't take them with us; we can only enjoy them for what they are.

Time afforded me the opportunity to get past the initial excitement of seeing them, a sort of vacation mentality, and to move toward a deeper appreciation of what a treasure the horses are. Much of what they do and what they are like can only be learned over time, as they favor some of the more remote and unseen sections of the beach: the uninhabited areas, including the maritime forests. The times that I could sit back and observe them where they knew they were alone was something quite special, and I came to see that they have different behaviors when entirely away from human civilization as compared to within it.

One of the biggest takeaways is how much we as a society think we know about horses, when it appears to not be true. I have spent time with those who own horses and ride them, and the horse I see in a pasture with a saddle on it is nothing like the horse I see wandering free on the beach. The difference is so stark that it drew me to not even like horses in the beginning, as I had made my opinion based upon domesticated horses.

It is hard to put into words, though over time I felt as though I developed an understanding of them as a group. There were many days when both my wife and I would have an intuition that today the horses would come out, or today they would be nowhere to be seen. Sometimes they were calm and peaceful, and other times the herd was anxious, due to any number of factors. The lead stallion in each group seemed to be the one to pay attention to, as though he was offering or withholding permission for my presence. His look was almost always authoritative, and if a person was listening, they knew where they stood in the matter.

There is a strictly enforced county ordinance about remaining 50 feet from the horses, a product of keeping the horses and the humans safe from a variety of factors. I will get into that a bit more in a future chapter, though I did find the rule tempting to break at times. My grandfather suggested against it, advising: "all it takes is once." I was dismissive of his advice internally, only to narrowly miss a full on stampede of six horses, with barely enough time to escape even though I was farther than the law required. Another time, I was down in a dune photographing a horse standing some distance on top of a dune, only to find another sneak up from behind and decide to declare war on the other stallion. While he did no harm, the look on his face suggested that I best remove myself from the situation.

Part of why I bring the distance ordinance up is that a wild horse is not a domesticated horse. There seems to be a temptation to treat what is wild as tame, and in so doing, that progressively works to remove the wild nature of things. It would be like seeing raw untamed ocean, and deciding to build piers and break walls; it would still be the ocean, though it would not be the same as its natural state. The whole experience is hinged upon having wild horses in an accessible place, and the fact that we want to get so close so as to risk the raw nature of things is indicative, in my opinion, of how starved we are of such things. The fact there is only one place to see the wild horses, living with humans, on the beach, is a real loss for society as a whole.

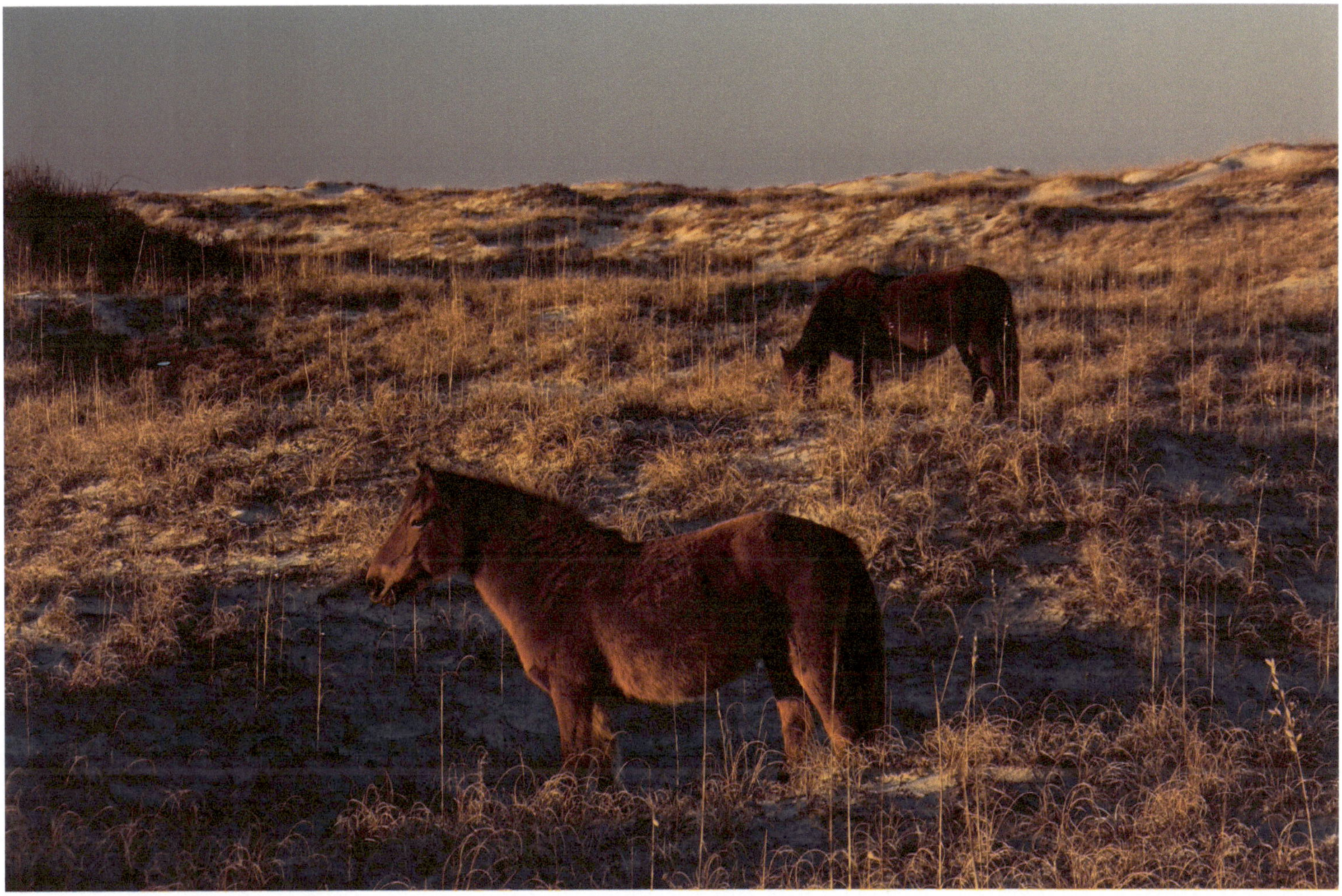

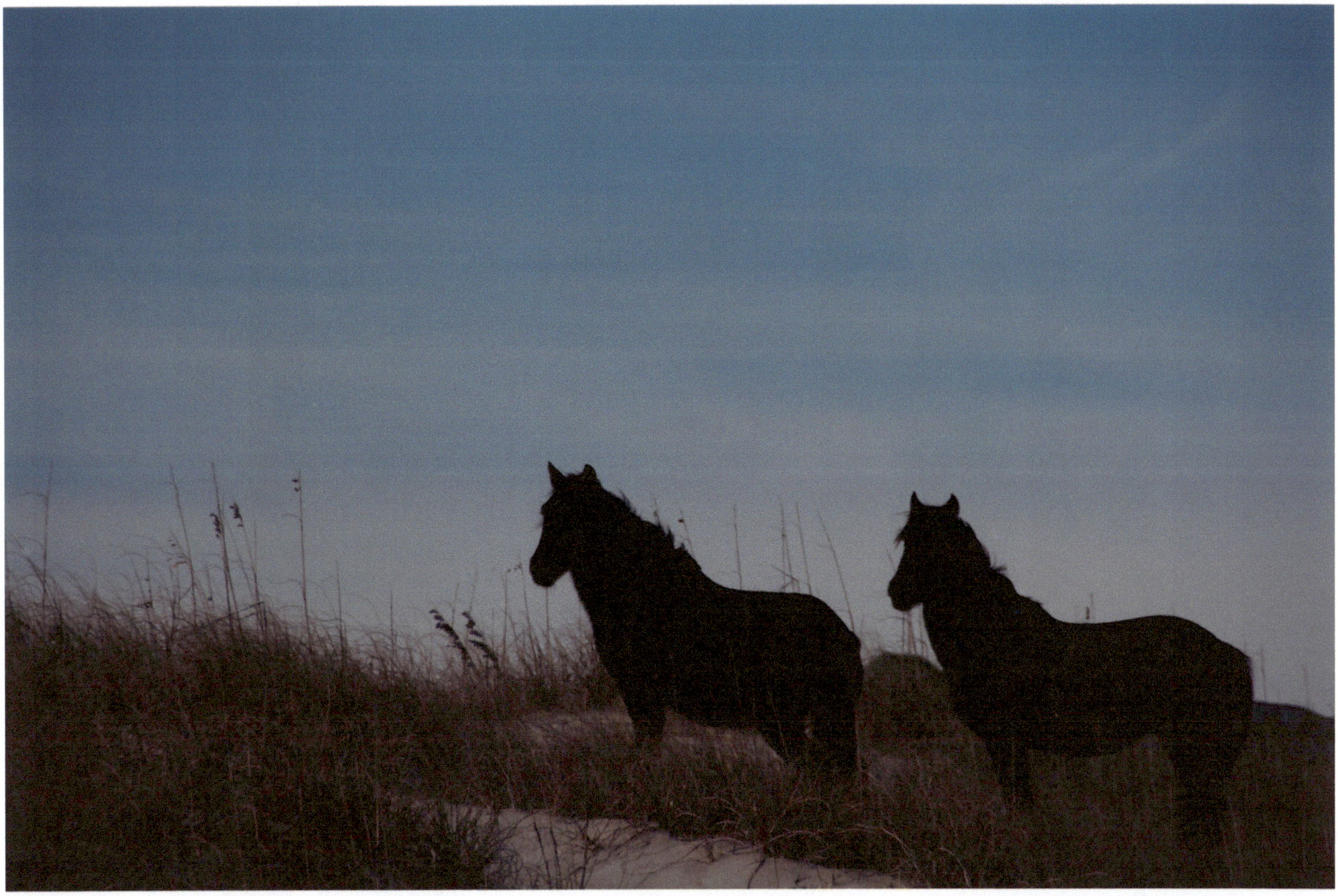

HORSE PHOTOGRAPHY TIPS

For the purposes of this section, I am making the assumption that it is desired to be able to take photographs in a style similar to what appears in this book. Each person is different, and will see different things. There is nothing more compelling than one's own artistic taste, so I encourage you to follow your instinct and try new things.

The first thing to consider before even starting is the background. I find that random people, houses, cars, and other human intrusions are not pretty; thus, I position myself so that the horses are between me and something natural, like the ocean. Most amateurs do not give this any thought.

Lighting is a secondary concern. While the sun may be pretty to the human eye, it usually makes a terrible companion in photographs, streaking and bleaching the entire thing out. The best angles are perpendicular to the sun, as shadows provide depth. Looking into the sun is a mortal sin, and looking directly away can be a bit flat, unless it is sunrise or sunset. Overcast skies are a challenge to work with as the horse is dark and the sky is extremely bright. The less sky the better in these circumstances. Otherwise, the only solution is to do some computerized processing with the image to reduce the bleached sky look.

For any serious photography, I recommend a DSLR camera. These are the type with detachable lenses, as opposed to point-and-shoot or camera phone varieties. While the technology for everyday photography has gotten better, options to do things differently than what comes out of the box are limited.

A polarizer is highly valuable at the coast if you will be including extensive backgrounds in the image. A polarizer screws on to the front of the lens and can be rotated so as to select which light can enter the lens. A polarizer will only allow one light direction in, so it does act like sunglasses for the camera. More importantly, it can eliminate reflections on water, deepen skies, reduce reflections on horses' fur, and make green foliage more resilient. For photographs where extensive zooming is used, polarizers

ABOVE:

Cranky stallions during a cold snow storm.

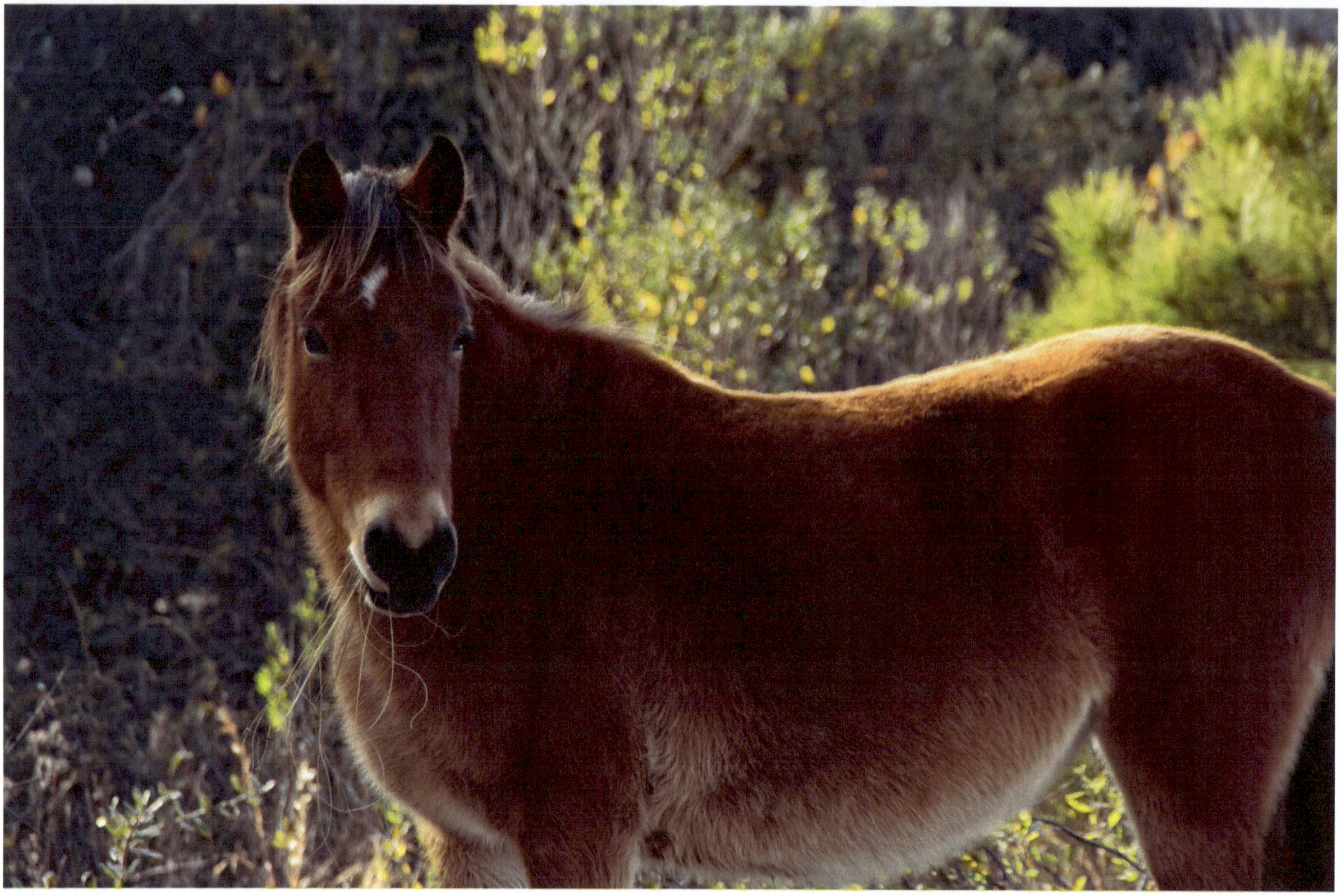

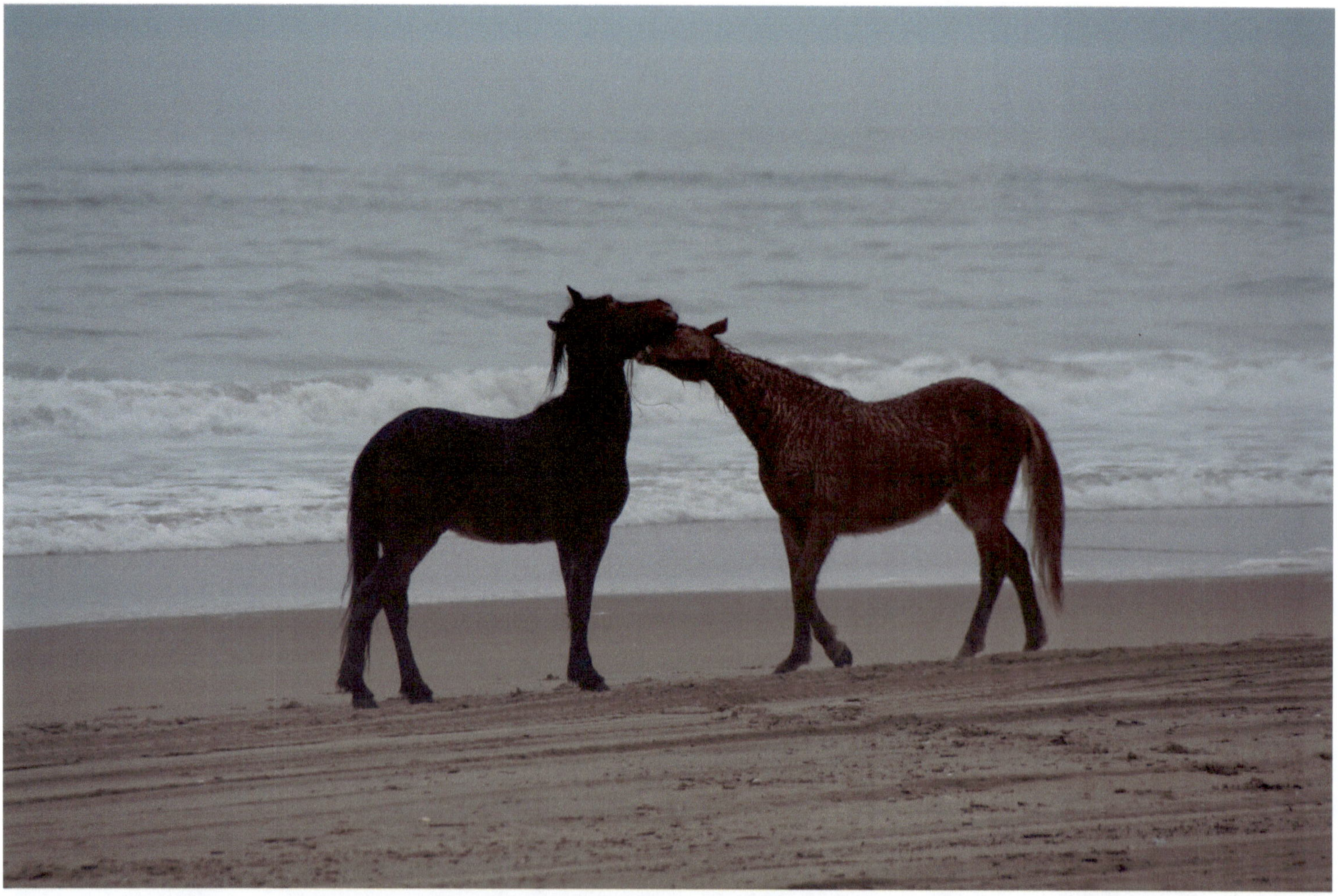

lose their utility to some extent and are not always needed.

I found that my telephoto zoom lens got extensive use at the coast. I normally shoot wide-angle photography, and found that the horse quickly gets lost. Rarely was a wide-angle image useful in conveying the scene; rather, it seemed to clutter it with unnecessary details. To best capture the detail of what horses are doing, and to avoid getting a citation for violating the 50-foot rule, a zoom lens is required.

The most common pose for the horses is eating, followed by trudging down the beach. If you're there for a few days or a week, the glee of seeing the horses will cause even these activities to be exciting. Some of the most profound images I find are when the horse is gazing into your camera. Ten percent of the time, they are looking around, whereas 90 percent of the time, they are head down in the grass. Generally, they will lift their heads to look at you when you first arrive, and that is your easiest window to get them looking. Otherwise, I suggest staking out a semi-hidden, non-threatening location, and waiting very, very patiently to catch them doing natural things.

If you have trouble finding the horses, then I suggest doing a lot of driving. They can't venture outside of a defined area, so it is a matter of driving the beach or the secondary access roads to see them. If you're there on a quiet day, sometimes I find that if I stop and listen, I'll hear them whinny, and then I start scouting for tracks in the sand. The deeper side of the footprint points in the direction where they are going, and the age of the footprints can be determined by their fresh look, whether they have been rained on, drifted over, or driven on. The footprints don't last more than a few days.

One of the most valuable ways to get good photos is to try what you think will work, go home, download the photos, and then realize that the idea didn't pan out. That is what happens in the beginning of every single book project of mine, no matter how well thought out the idea was, and I find myself recalibrating my approach and trying something else. Determination is the key to amazing images.

The Future of the Horses

If it were not for the concerted effort of concerned citizens and the Corolla Wild Horse Fund, the horses would be on a steady decline, and would eventually disappear from the Outer Banks altogether. A registered breed that is critically endangered (less than 100 breeding mares), they are under constant assault from a variety of human influences. If we left the island altogether, they would manage well except for a few factors.

The first human influence is the fact that humans share the habitat, and do so poorly sometimes. Four horses have been confirmed dead as a result of automobile collisions from 2007 to 2014, and two more are suspected of having been hit by a car prior to their deaths. Four have been confirmed dead due to colic, which is when they are fed human food that they cannot digest, and they die a terribly painful death. From 2001 to 2014, 7 have been shot. Another died of complications due to a roofing nail piercing into bone, despite $5,000 spent to attempt to save her. A multitude of horses have acquired colic from human causes and survived, at a cost of $500 per treatment. Each necropsy to determine cause of death costs $1,000, and if a horse is found too late, cause of death cannot be determined, thus it stands to reason that many more have died from human causes, though cannot be proven.

The second factor is an odd political structure in Corolla, resulting in next to no Corolla-based political influence on the decision-making process that governs where the horses live. There are few local voting permanent residents, as second homeowners own property though cannot vote in Currituck County. While many of those second homeowners care deeply about the horses, their voice is limited. Thus, as of this writing, the elected officials governing where the horses live are all based on the mainland, a one-hour drive through Dare County to get there. That political structure simply creates a situation where incentives are not lined up in the horses' favor, despite hundreds of thousands of people who visit the horses and love them.

On its own, the third factor is money. There is a fair amount of undeveloped land on the 4x4 beach, and economics dictates that it will always be more profitable to build a giant hotel and sell the development than to think of the long-term cash cow that is the horses themselves. While it would make

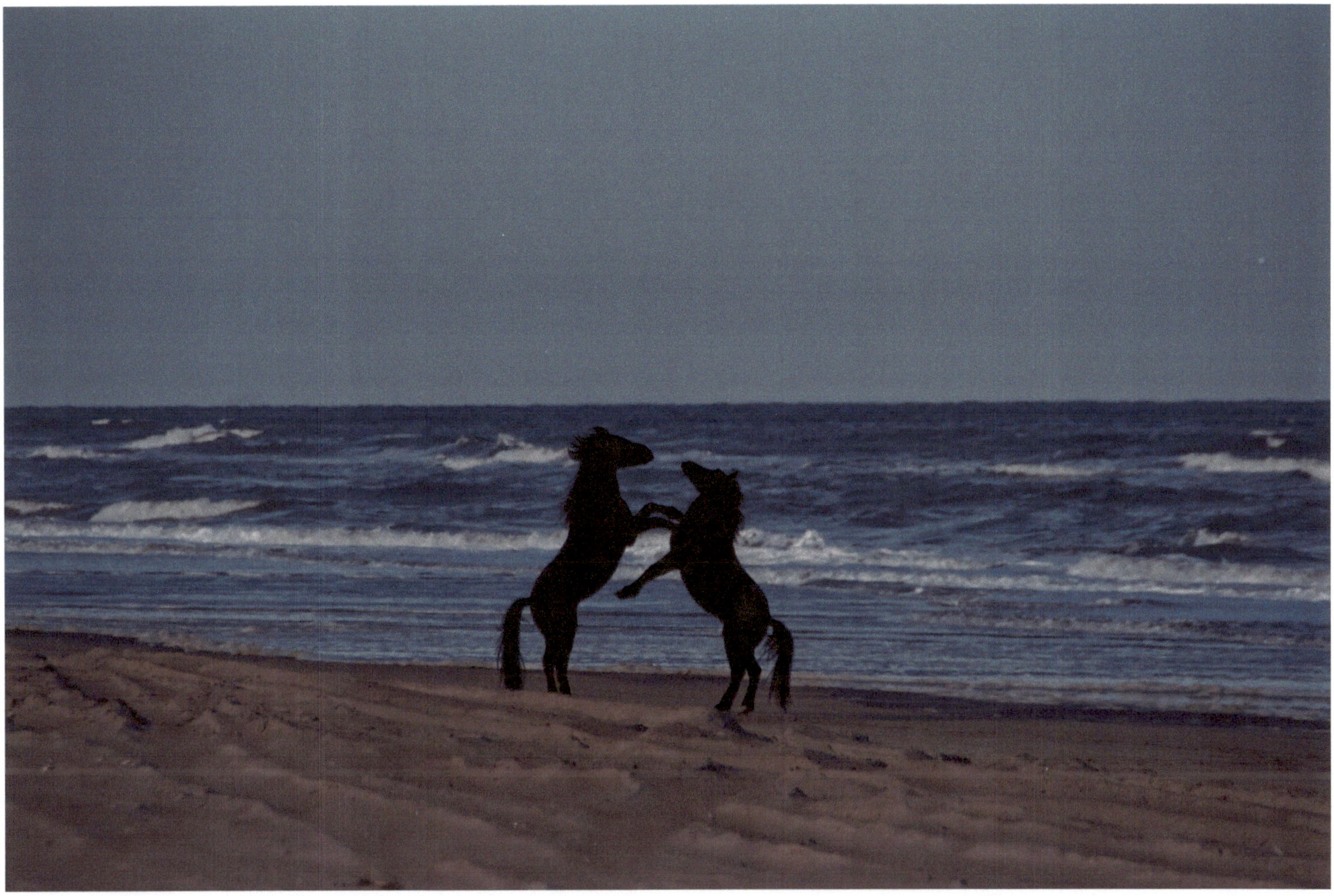
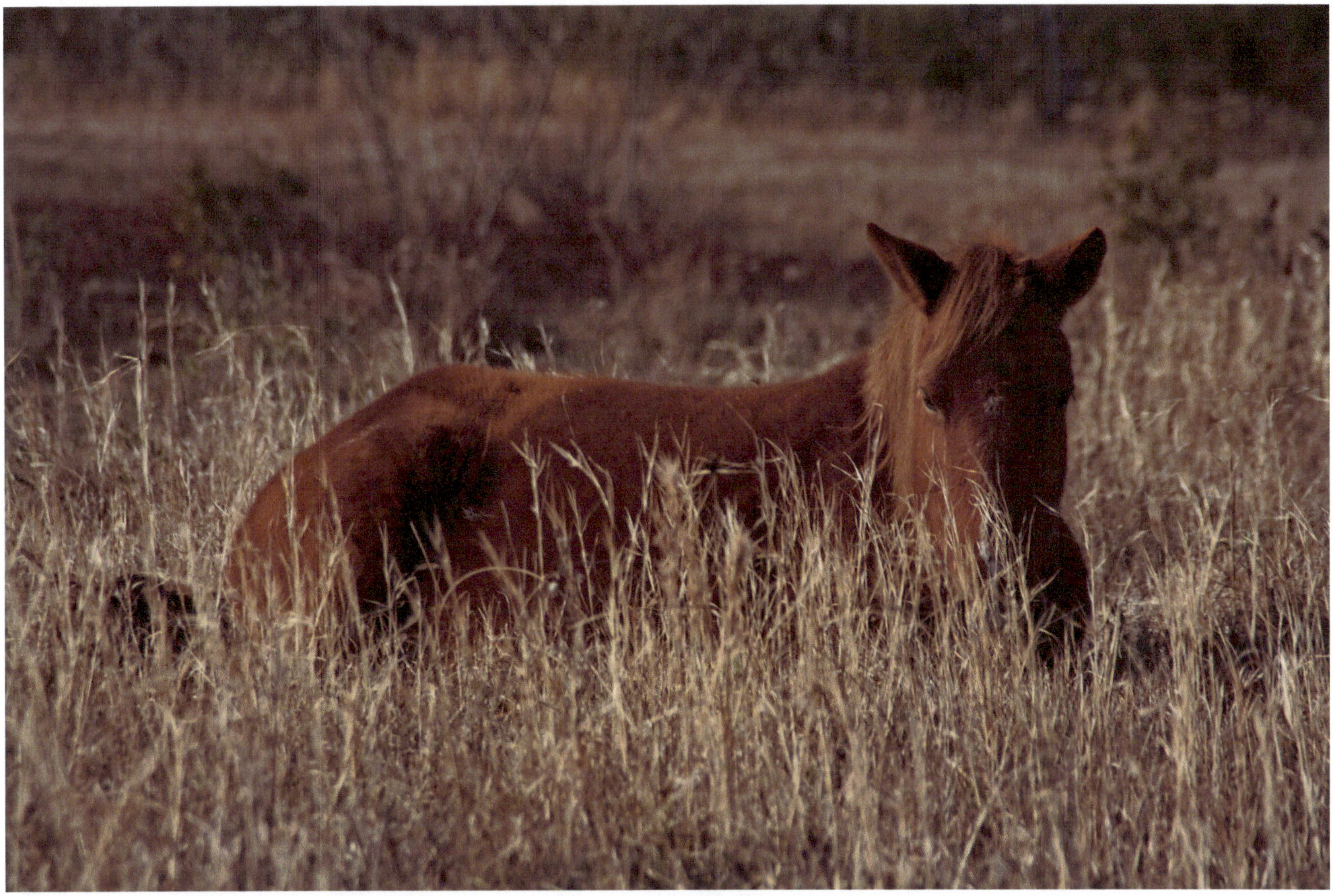

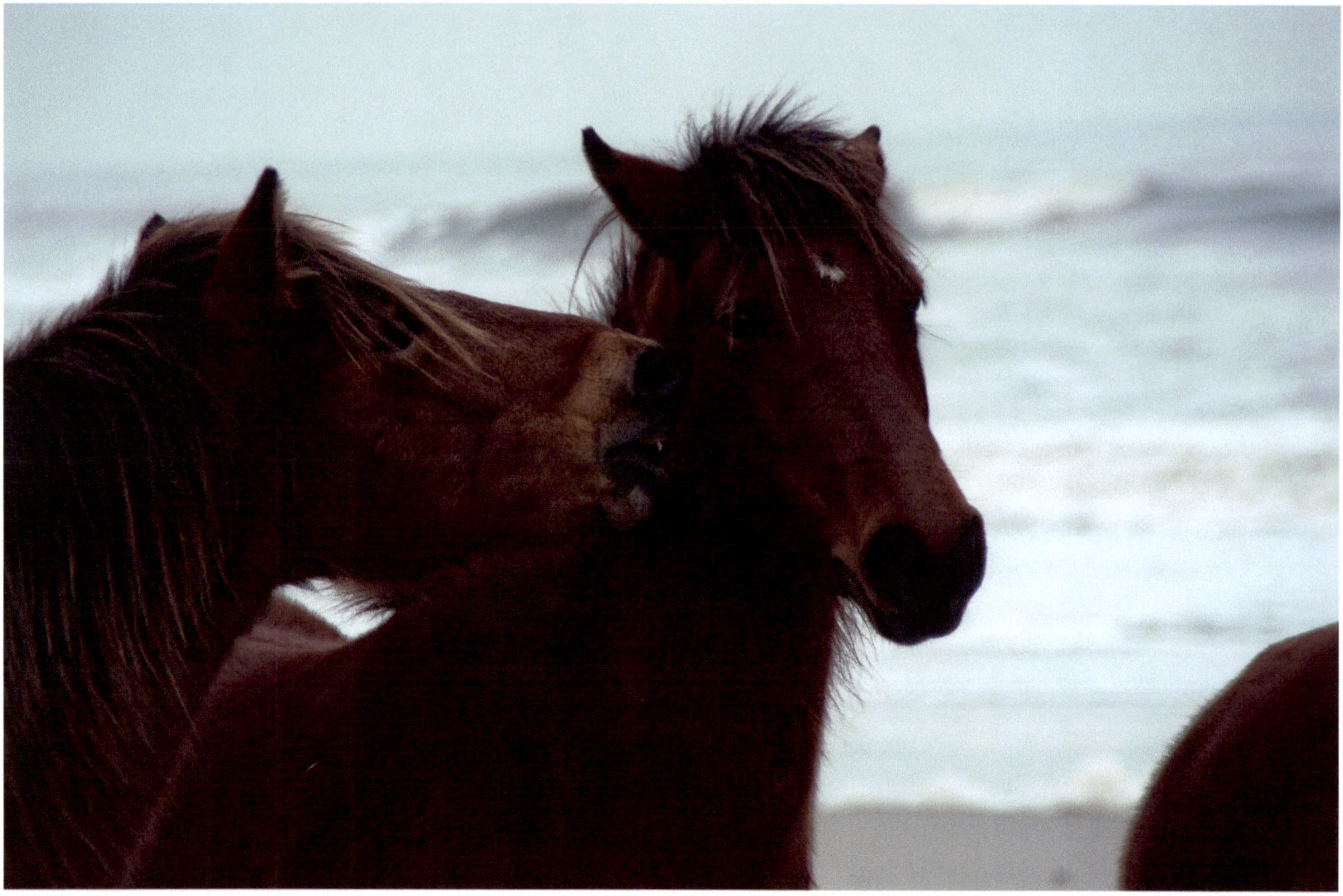

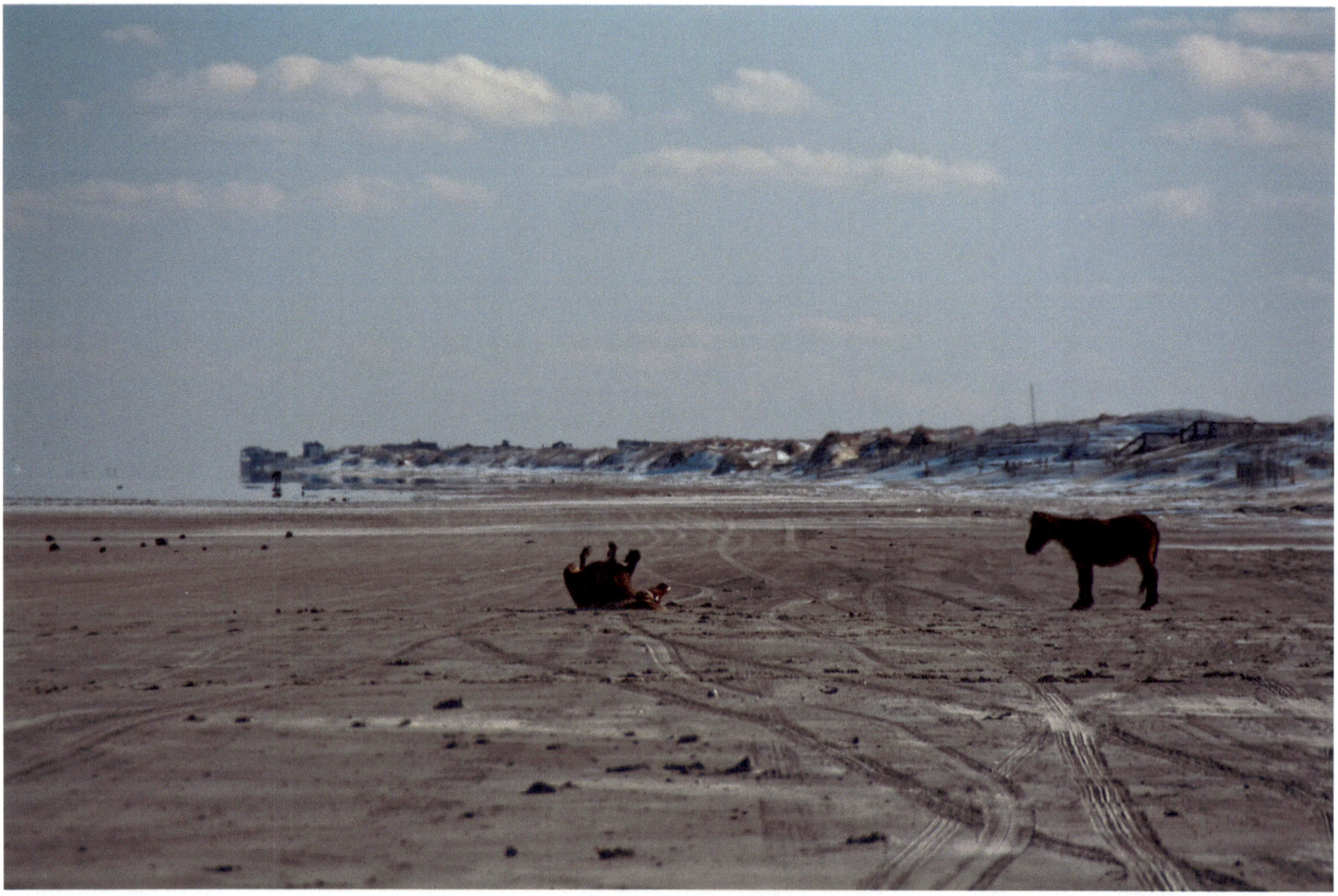

some money for some individuals to introduce sizable development, it would also be one step closer to pushing the horses out. As of this writing, there is litigation pending attempting to force zoning changes to allow commercial development. If it were to be successful, more would follow, with devastating effects to the room available for the horses.

The fact that NC 12 goes onto the beach is a result of the US Fish and Wildlife Service owning the first mile and a half of the land at the end of the pavement. By agreement with the state of NC and Currituck County, the highway is permitted to go onto the beach for access to private property. Fish & Wildlife has labeled the horses as a pest, and there have been land swaps proposed. They also have fenced off acreage, denying the horses access. Were Fish & Wildlife to give up the land to another entity, it might allow for a road, or worse, they could deny access to the horses altogether. Combine the economic factors of turning the 4x4 section into Myrtle Beach, coupled with weak local representation, and the beach we all love to visit may entirely disappear as we know it, along with the horses.

When I set out to spend the winter with the horses and write a book about it, I did not want to get involved in the threats to them. I just wanted to portray them as they were. In fact, I did not speak to really anyone during my photography process, I simply observed what I saw, researched what made the 4x4 beach what it was, and drew some conclusions about how the place does not look sustainable. After conversing with many locals, law enforcement, and the Corolla Wild Horse Fund, I found that my personal conclusions lined up with on-the-ground reality. The horses need protection, they need room, and they need legislative involvement to make sure of it.

A similar story happened over two decades ago with the wild horses on Shackleford Banks. They would have been removed had Congress not intervened, and the simple legislation that passed named a non-profit as official caretakers of those horses. The model worked then, and it needs to be replicated in Corolla. Hopefully by the time you read this book, legislation will have cleared the Senate and received the President's signature, making the Corolla Wild Horse Fund the official federal caretaker of these horses, preserving them for the indefinite future.

Even more than having caretakers, the horses need space. Space costs money, and the solution is to permanently set aside land for their use, doing so in a way that compensates existing

landowners fairly, by purchasing undeveloped land and setting it aside; nobody has to be kicked out. Just as our National Parks are worth great sums of money and have been set aside for our national enjoyment, it is my belief that the horses need the same. People from countless states come to enjoy them, and they belong available to the nation for the indefinite future. They are the only wild horses you can live with on any beach in this country, and it would be shame to let short-term interests push them out. We would regret it if we lost them.

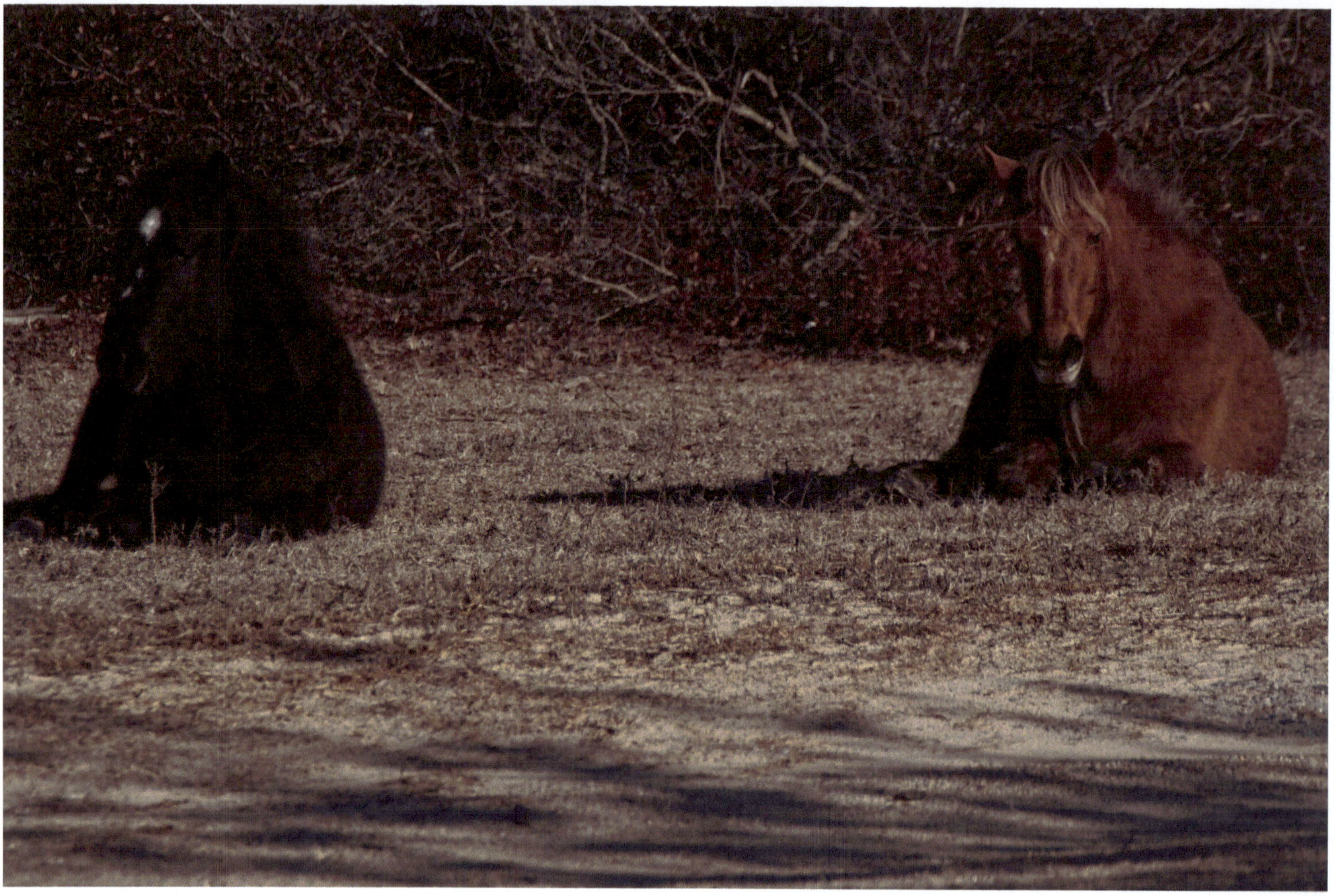

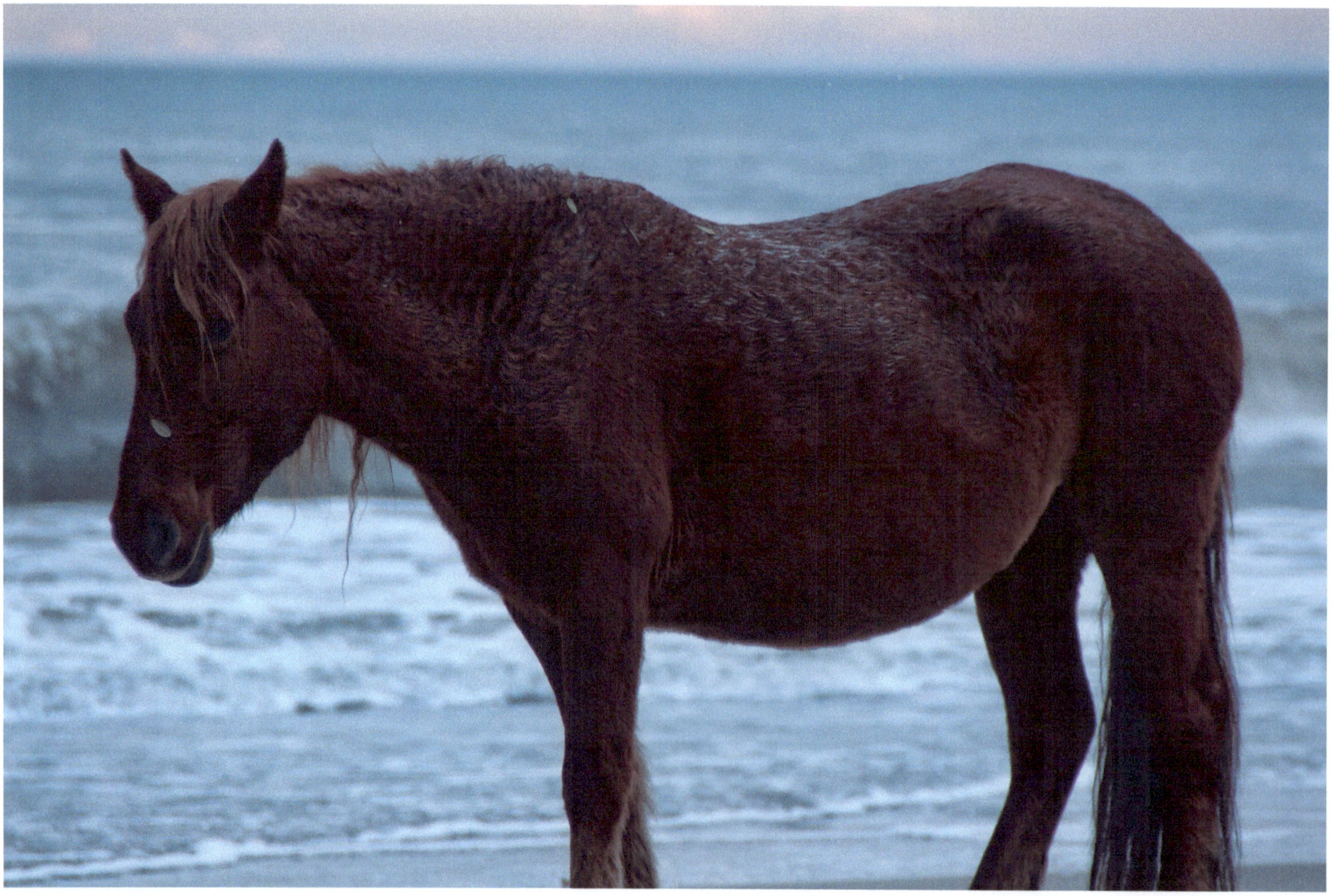

Above: *Rare nap with head laid down.* **Below:** *Eating some sea oats during one of many snow storms.*

BELOW: *Scratching an itch.*

ABOVE: *Fox walking away after trying to play with sleeping horse.*

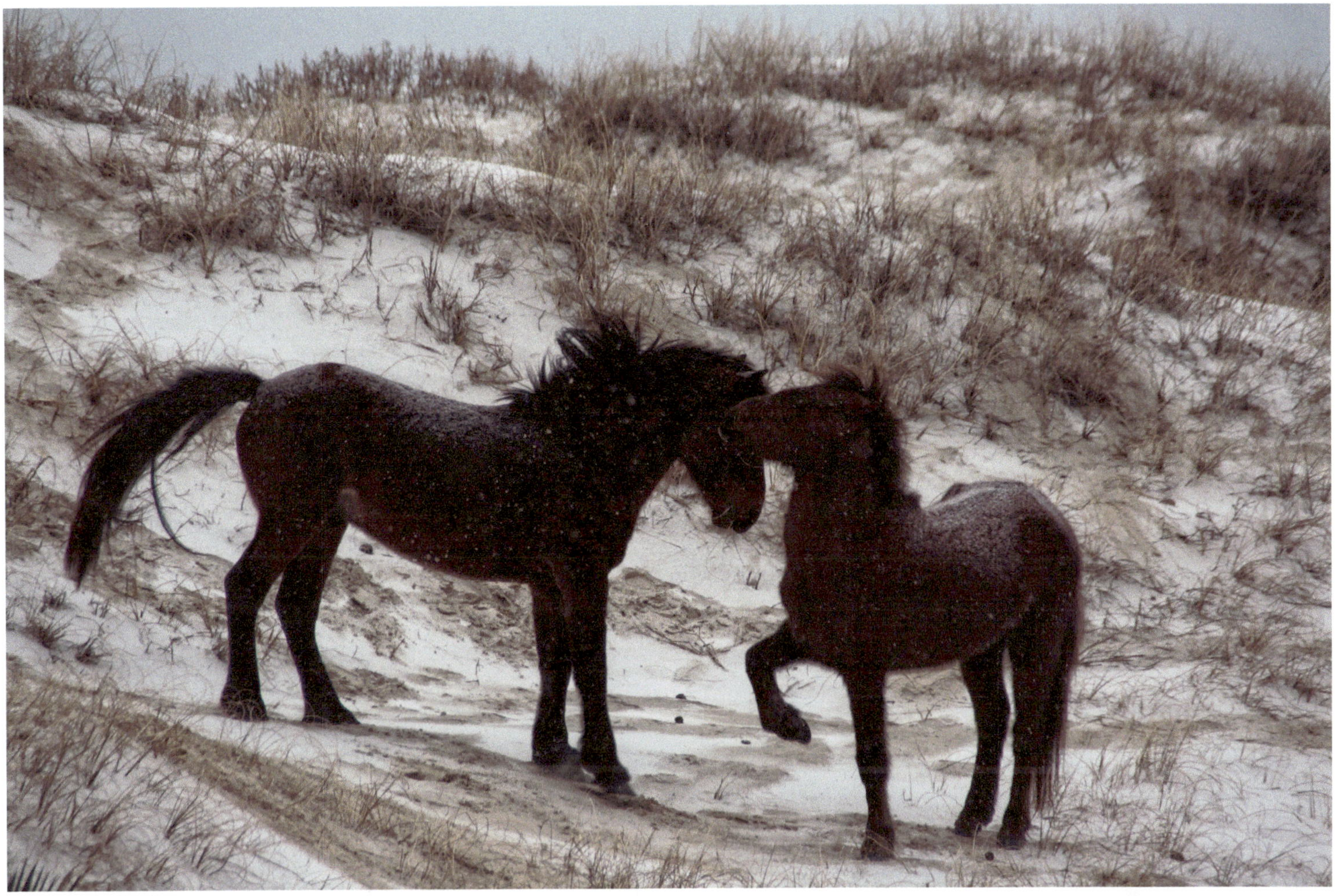

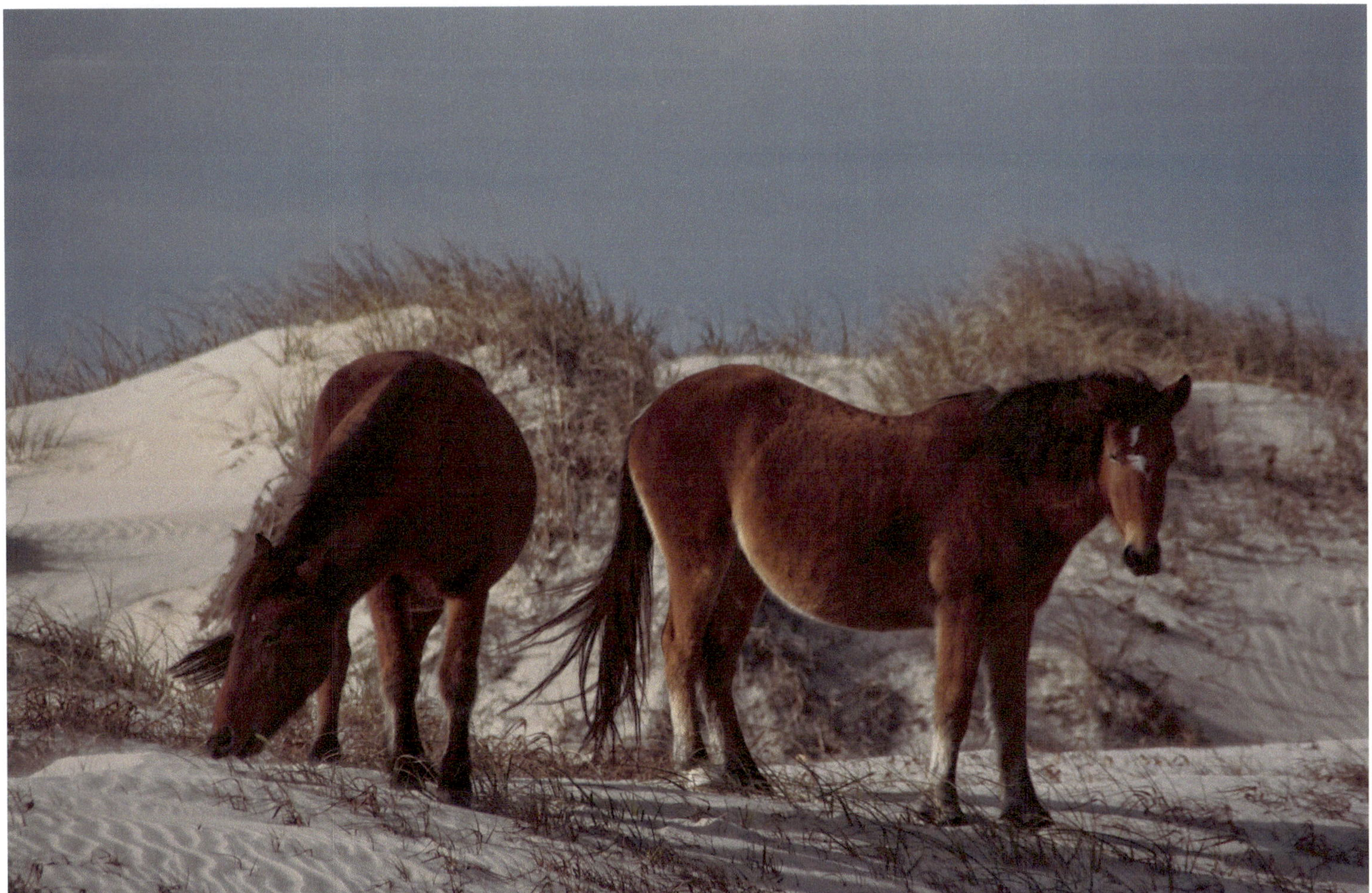

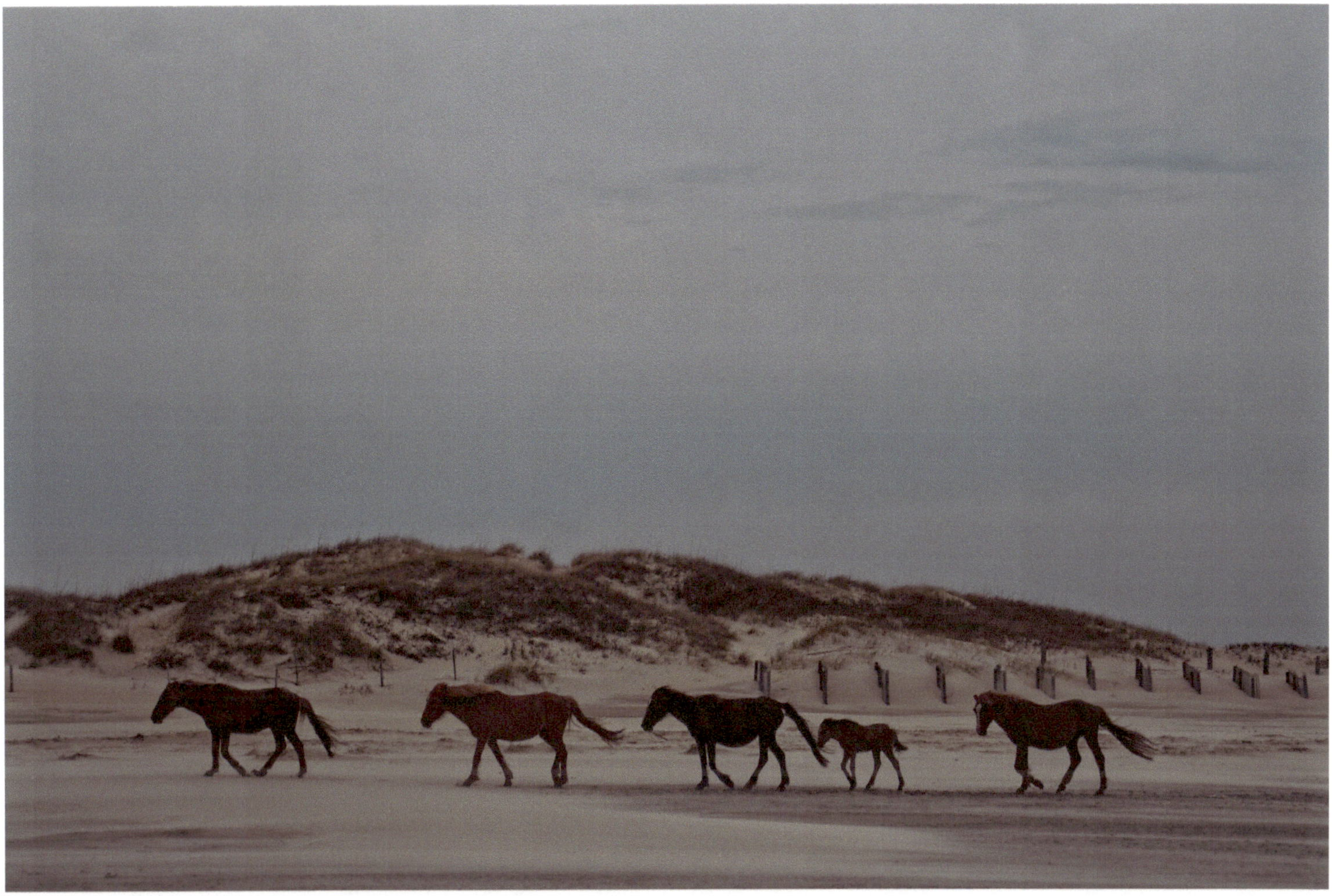

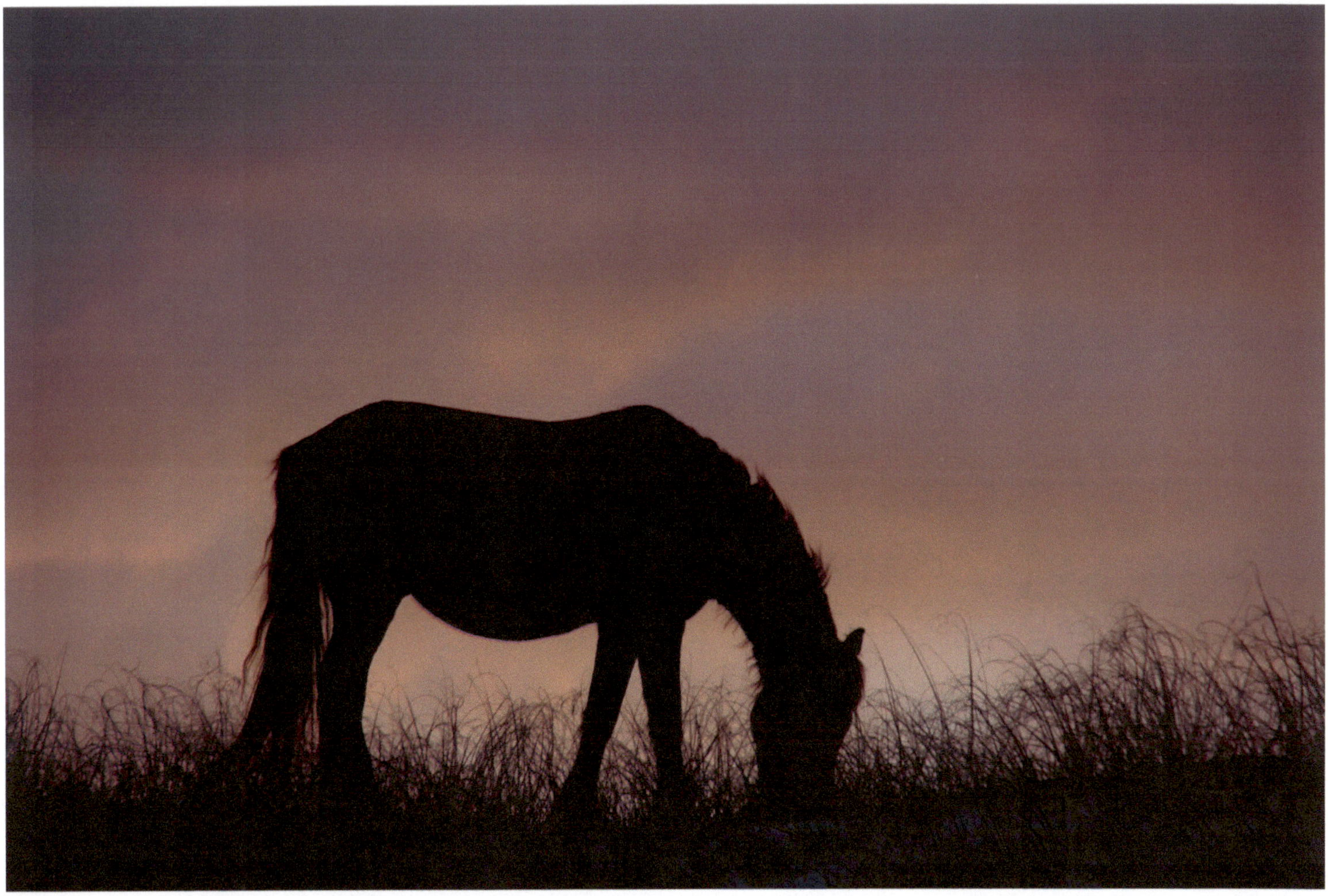

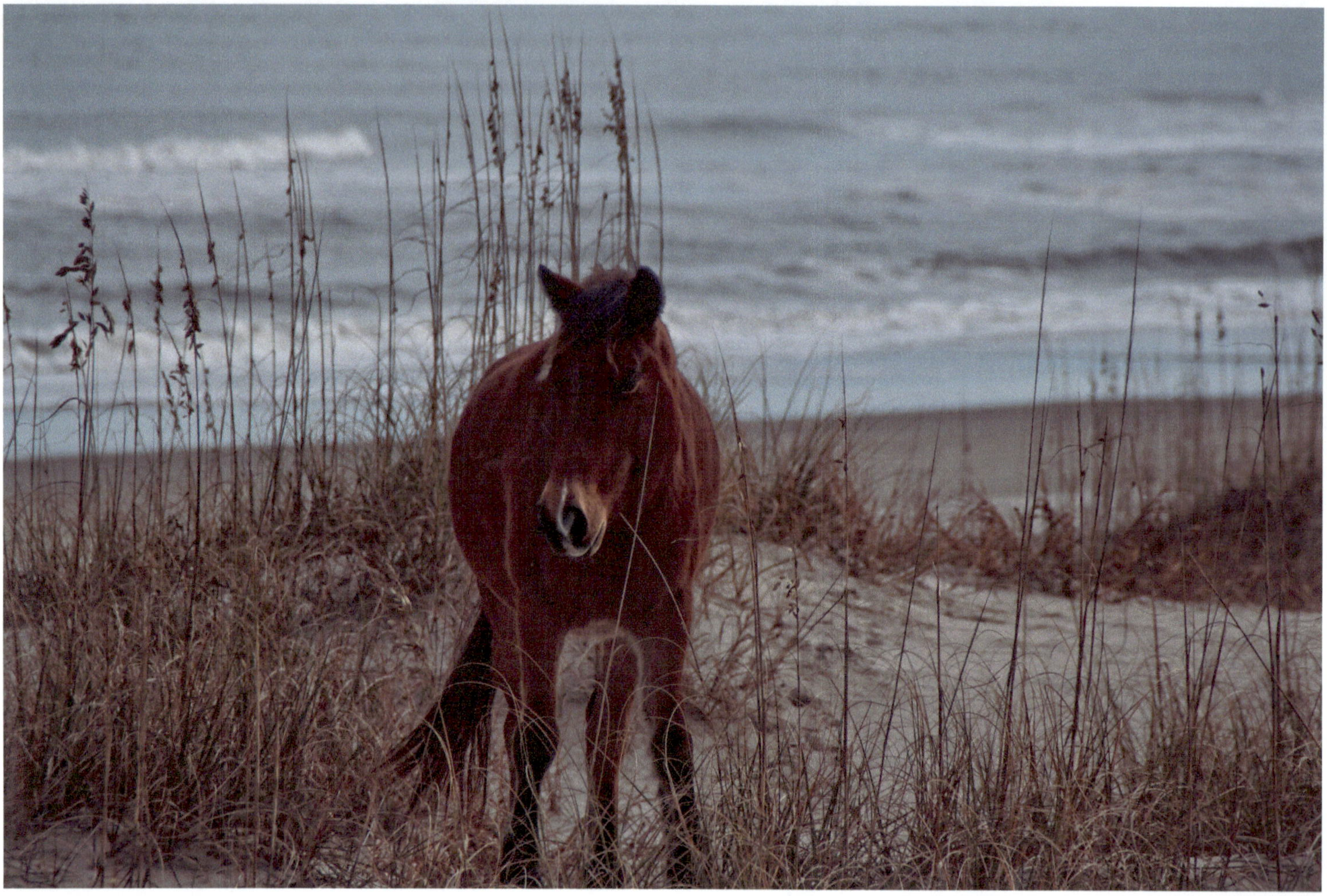

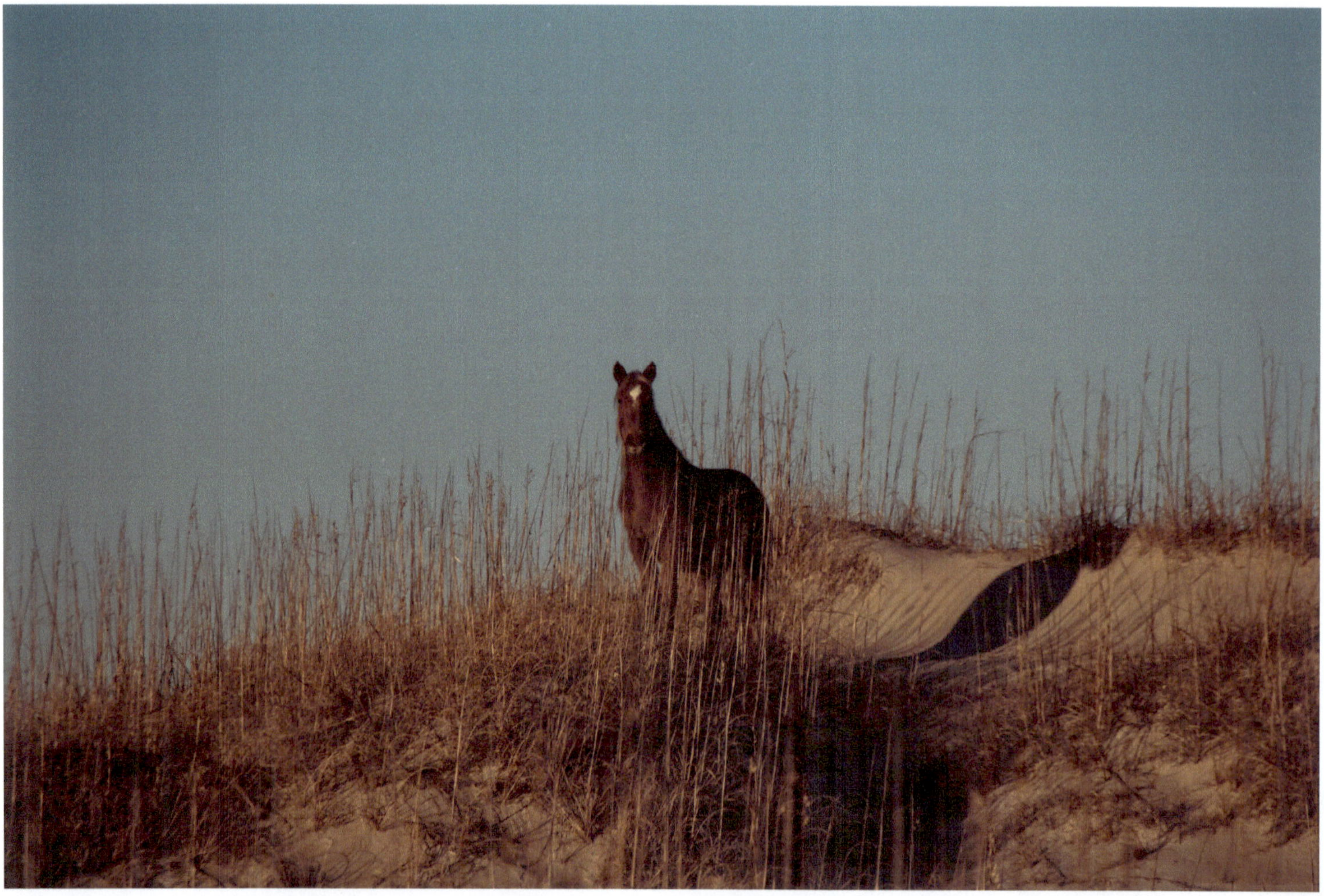

Above: *Mares disputing with each other.*

ABOVE: *Scratching an itch.*

BELOW: *Seemingly aimless trudging.*

BELOW: *Digging for grass after an ice storm.*

ABOVE: *Unknown to me, this horse was gazing not at the sunset, but at an angry stallion creeping up behind me.*

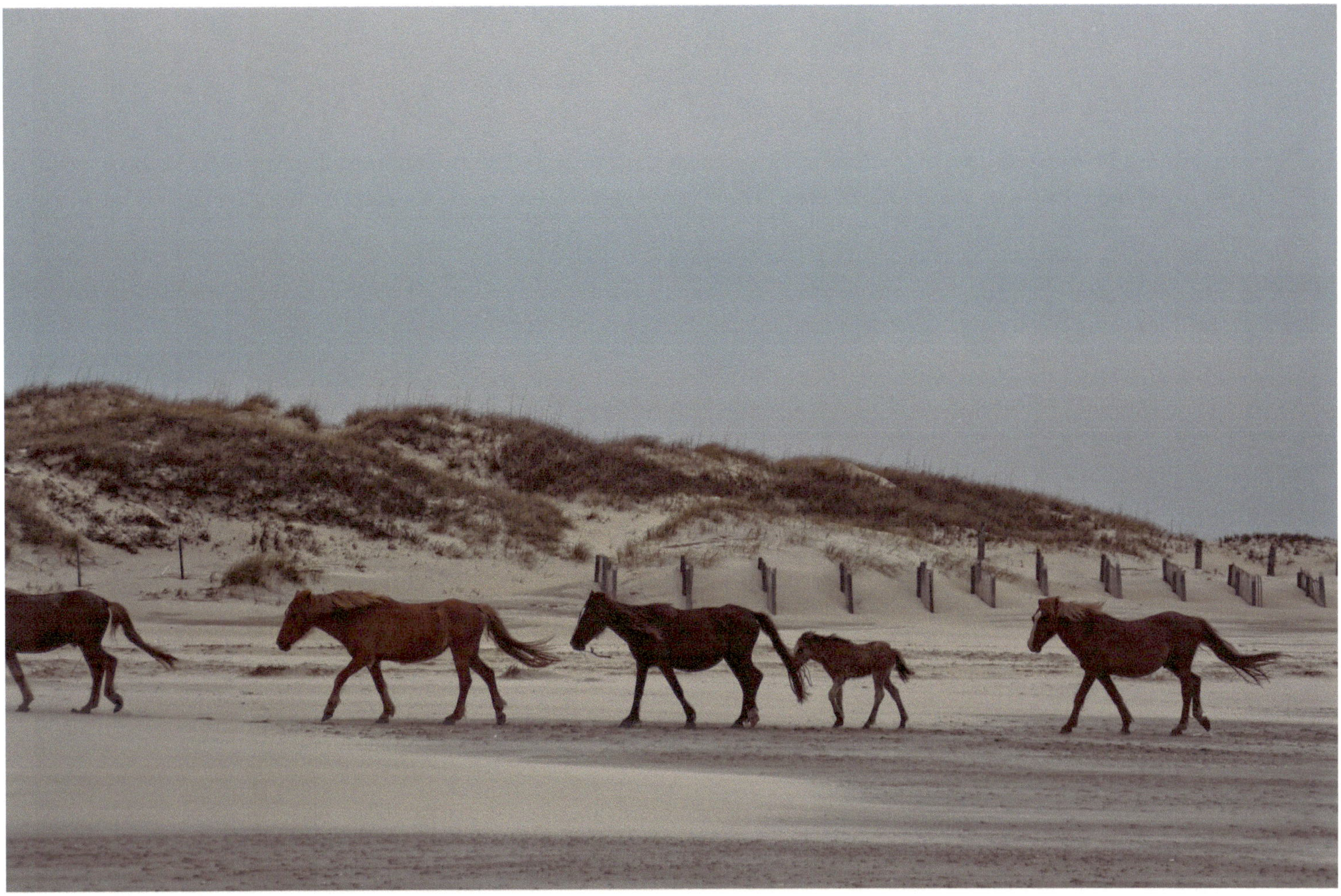

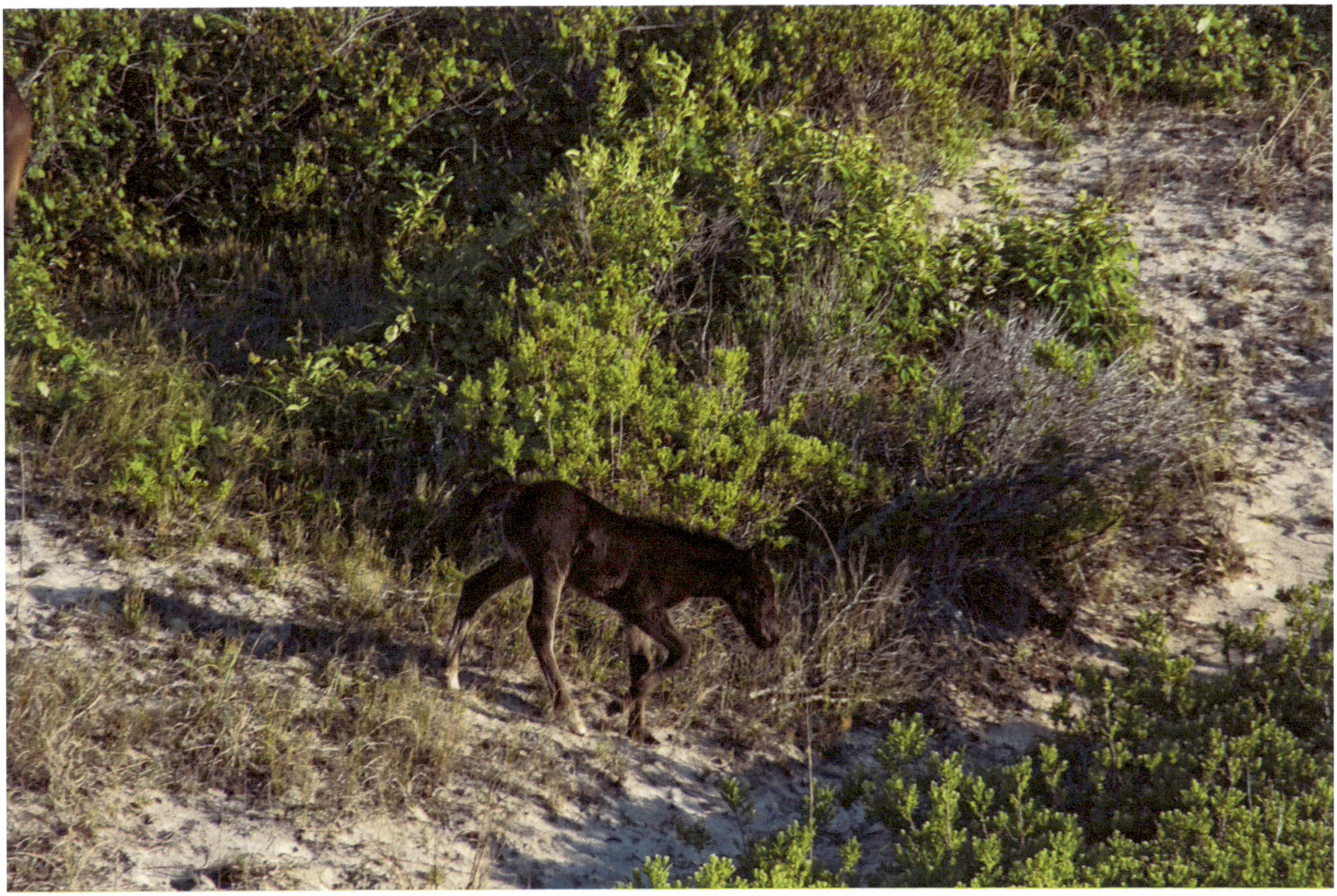

Visiting the Horses

Visiting the horses requires the willingness to take a paid tour, or the possession of a 4x4 vehicle. *It is very hard to get there as a pedestrian, if 4x2 vehicle parking is needed.* Here is some information to ensure you and your vehicle are still in one piece afterward:

- Only 4x4 vehicles with a direct drive axle work on the sand. All wheel drive with fluid transfer clutches cannot handle the torque that sand will place on it, at the risk of destroying the AWD system.

- Clearance should be that of a standard SUV/pickup truck or higher. Smaller vehicles like Honda CRVs and Toyota Rav4 are too low and will get hung up in deep ruts.

- Lower all four tires to 15 to 20 PSI before entering the beach. It is marked on the right on the map where to pull off and do so. Driving a few miles on the tires on pavement decreases gas mileage at worst; however, be cautious as stopping distance is increased and curves are less tight. Tires can be re-inflated at the nearest gas station for a dollar or less as of this writing. While vehicles can drive on the beach without deflation, it is hard on the transmission and dramatically increases chances of getting stuck. Further, low pressure is a requirement for deep sand, dune ramps, and ruts. *If everyone lowered their tire pressure, there would not be deep, almost impassable ruts.*

- Low tread tires are better. Rugged off-road tires dig down into the sand and make more of a problem. If you have aggressive tires, deflating to lower PSI is an absolute must, and avoid deep sand. The most beastly trucks with monster tires seemed to be the ones that got stuck the most.

- Do not slam on the brakes unless you're about to hit something, as the vehicle will sink into the sand.

- Never, ever spin the tires. All that accomplishes is digging a hole, and once in the hole, it is very hard to get out. If tires are at low pressure, 4x4 engaged, and spinning is the result, call a tow or get a shovel and dig a ramp to back out of the problem. Digging deeper makes it worse.

- Transmissions are not designed for spinning tires in sand while stuck, or rocking under high torque. The fluid will heat up and boil, coming out of the dipstick, landing on the exhaust manifold and will start the vehicle on fire. It is quite common. If stuck, get some help to get out. I suggest checking web reviews, as not every local company is well recommended.

- Do not drive in salt water. It destroys the vehicle and, if deep enough, people seem to stall out their vehicles regularly.

- There are stumps in many sections of the beach. Sometimes they are buried, other times the ocean digs them out so that people can drive into them. Some of them are in the water (another reason not to drive into the ocean).

- If you see a sports car, a 4x2 vehicle, or a vehicle without deflated tires on the sand, it does not mean that it will work for you. Each vehicle, person, and circumstance is different. Remember, many people are just plain dumb, and that Camaro will probably be found buried in the sand later in the day.

- If the driver and vehicle have skill and experience on the sand, it is possible to be flexible with some of these suggestions, though not all of them. It is easier to take some precautions than deal with a stuck, burnt, or washed away vehicle.

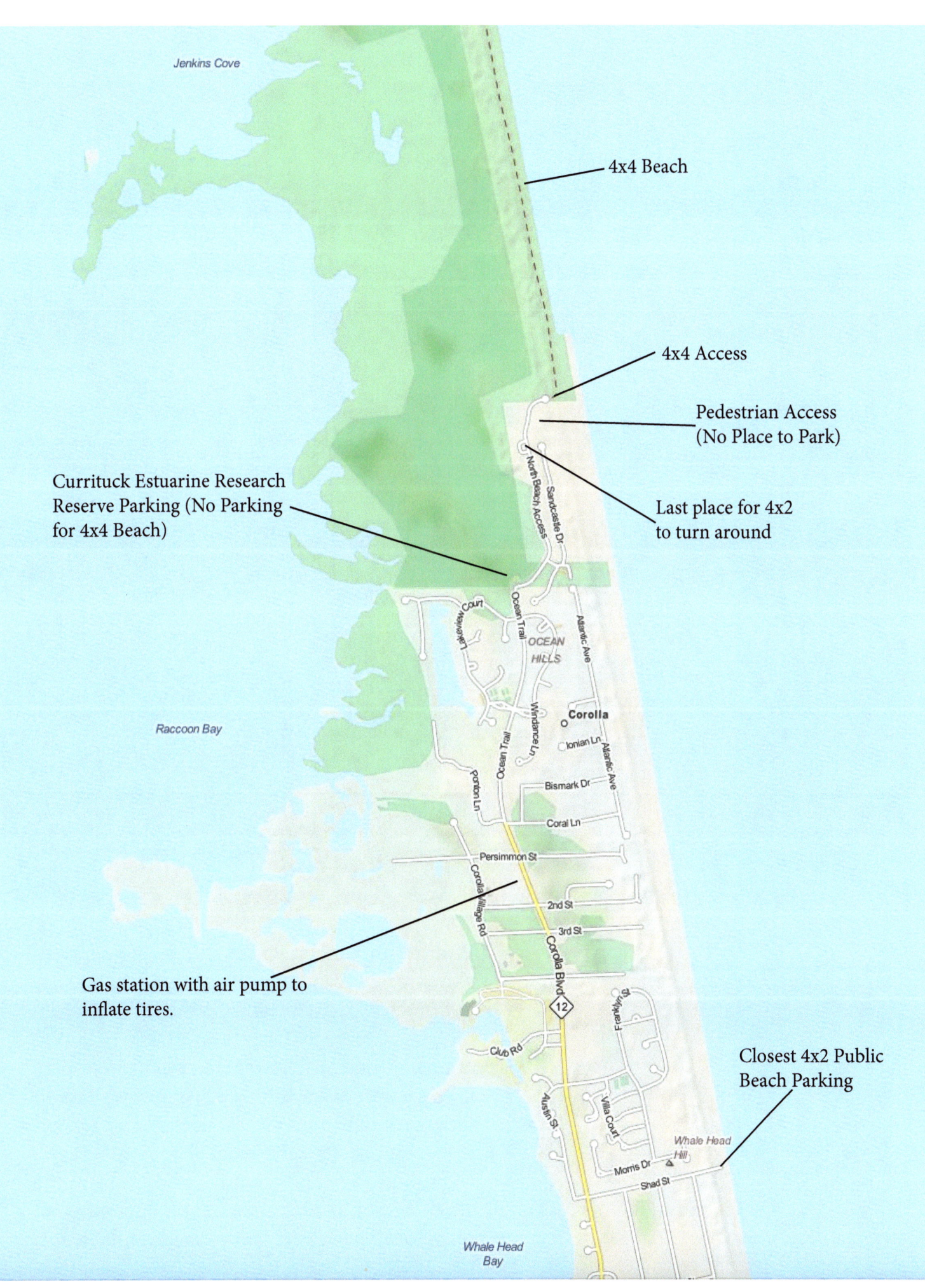

More Books by the Author

Photo Credit: Adam Romer

With a thirst for new and interesting perspectives, Garrett Fisher is perpetually adventure flying, undertaking a variety of projects at any given moment. Currently, he lives on an airpark in Wyoming outside of Yellowstone, where he is working on a host of book projects, two of which will focus on Grand Teton National Park and Yellowstone National Park. He blogs about the flights he takes to explore and document things from the air, providing an abundance of photographs and maps on his website at www.garrettfisher.me.

www.ingramcontent.com/pod-product-compliance
Lightning Source LLC
Chambersburg PA
CBHW042013150426

43196CB00002B/33